Making It In The Business

Overcoming Obstacles and Achieving Your Goals In The Entertainment Industry

Making It In The Business

Overcoming Obstacles and Achieving Your Goals In The Entertainment Industry

Andrea Hill Ph.D. MFT

The Center Press

MAKING IT IN THE BUSINESS: Overcoming Obstacles and Achieving Your Goals In The Entertainment Industry by Andrea Hill Ph.D. MFT

Copyright © 2001 by Andrea Hill Ph.D.

Published by:
The Center Press P.O. Box 6936 Thousand Oaks, CA 91360-6936

Library of Congress Cataloging-In-Publication Data
    Hill, Andrea, 1946-
    Making it in the business: overcoming obstacles and reaching your goals in the
    entertainment industry / by Andrea Hill.
        p.cm.
    Includes bibliographical references and index.
    ISBN 1-889198-07-2
    1. Entertainers--Mental health. 2. Entertainers-- Psychology.
    3. Entertainers--Job Stress 4. Persistence. 5. Performing Arts--Psychological aspects.
    6. Success in business--Psychological aspects. I Title.

RC451.4.E57 H55 2001
616.89'0088'79—dc21   00-065685
                                                                     CIP

Cover design by Susan Shankin
Interior book design by Lindsay Artof
Printed By KNI

Printed and bound in the United States of America
10 9 8 7 6 5 4 3 2 1

For Lyle, the center of my life.

Acknowledgments

The creation of this book has been a very natural response to my years of working and sharing ideas with people in the entertainment industry. Each student, each client, has helped shape my ideas and helped me to form a philosophy.

My sincerest thanks and gratitude go to the following people:

To the actors, writers, singers, and other performers who wrote to me and trusted me with their questions and concerns about their careers and personal lives.

To the thousands of actors who have graced us with their talent and spirit at our acting workshops.

To the clients I have had the privilege of working with in my psychology practice.

To my publisher, Sue Artof, for her hours of effort, encouragement, and faith in the validity and value of this book.

To my friend, Mary Landroth, for her many hours of final editing.

To my friend and assistant, Richard St. James, for seeing to it that casting directors and agents had a copy of the manuscript to look at and comment upon.

To my dad, Andy DeCapite, who was at my side during every pursuit that interested me as a child, and who gave me every educational opportunity available so that I could pursue all of my interests as an adult.

And mostly...

To my husband, Lyle, for his strength, love, and devotion to me and for his enthusiastic encouragement with regard to the writing of this book and all the other projects that we have created and adventures we have enjoyed throughout the years.

Contents

Foreward

Acting: Profession or Lark

Historically, in most parts of the world, acting has been treated as a profession. Unfortunately, in the United States, many approach acting as something to do when all else fails. Many people who wish to pursue acting as a career believe that all they have to do is show up in New York or Hollywood, present themselves, and they will magically have a rewarding career financially and psychologically. This could not be farther from reality. If one pursues acting, it is an odyssey of work, and more work. It is imperative that the would-be actor study the classics, work with a recognized professional acting teacher, and among other requirements, pursue a formal education. Joining a theatre group is also a very wise thing to do. These are a few of the basics.

In addition, one must be mentally prepared to accept continual rejection. I have heard stars in films say, as they get close to a picture's wrap, "I wonder if I will ever work again." Andrea Hill lays out the obstacles and suggests the ways and means of achieving success in the profession of acting. It is never easy, but her advice lays it on the line, and can guide the neophyte as well as the seasoned performer towards a rewarding experience.

Mike Fenton, CSA
Television and Film Casting Director
Encino, California

I believe the enclosed text is a valuable tool in understanding the world of your fantasy. Not everyone in the casting office comprehends your dreams. Your brittleness is part of the dimension of acceptance and rejection. This book will assist performers in accepting the inner reliance of their creativity.

I like the fact that Andrea Hill's words will improve the actor's trust in himself and those he is auditioning for. I appreciate the simplicity of thoughts which are put forth. Take what you need and utilize these guidelines to the best of your ability for your artistic journey.

As a casting director, I am faithfully aware that the actor is a human and not a machine. Here is a book supporting my philosophy.

Eddie Foy III
Casting Director
Dick Clark Productions

Preface

If you work in the entertainment industry, or if you're a struggling actor, director, or screen writer looking for that important opportunity, you deal not only with the problems that life presents to all people, but you also face unique challenges that are created by being in show business. Many of you have left the security of your hometown in order to make your dreams happen, leaving family and friends wondering whether you're crazy! Some of you have walked away from job security and the life your parents expected you to live, to become the person you dream you can be. You are a risk-taker!

This book is for you and about you. Each chapter covers a letter I have received from someone like you. It's about finding the right agent, managing your performance anxiety and dealing with rejection. But this book also looks at deeper issues such as eating disorders resulting from the pressure to have the perfect body, how to help your relationship survive the long separations of location filming, recovery from drug addiction; it even explores whether you've chosen the right profession.

Because of my three careers as performer, acting coach, and therapist for actors at all levels from beginners to movie stars, I understand the business and all the thrills and disappointments that are part of it. The more you know about the nature of this industry, the better prepared you'll be to handle each experience, seize each opportunity, avoid painful mistakes and fully enjoy the whole process.

Introduction

I'll never forget Kevin, even though we only had one encounter. I was struck by his intensity and ambition. The night I met him, he expressed frustration and disappointment beyond anything he had ever felt before. When we were introduced at a private party, the hostess told him that I owned an acting school, *Weist-Barron-Hill, Acting for Television and Film*, and that I was also a psychotherapist specializing in work with people in the entertainment industry. Almost immediately he began looking around the room, trying to find a quiet corner, as far away from the music as possible, where we could talk. He hoped that I would understand his despair, and I did.

Kevin had been in the running for the starring role of an important major motion picture. It was predicted to become one of the most important movies of the decade. The director called him back several times and he was very encouraged. He knew he did a stirring performance at each callback. At the end, only one other actor was in contention for the role. But finally the other actor got the part. Kevin was very disappointed and it took weeks for him to recover from the loss. Eighteen months later the movie was released and became one of the highest grossing movies of all time. The actor who won the role has become a huge celebrity, respected all over the world for his truthful performance, admired for his "movie star" chemistry, and rewarded with offers of huge sums of money for his next picture. It was impossible for Kevin to avoid seeing what might have been his.

As Kevin told me his story, his face was filled with the pain of his loss. He believed that the opportunity of his life simply vanished. He felt in his heart that the moment was lost forever and he had missed the realization of his dream by a mere thread. As we talked, I saw a yearning, a longing for the opportunity that slipped through his fingers. He told me he drank too much and sometimes stayed in bed all day long. Sometimes he couldn't find a reason to go on. We talked for a long time and I know he felt understood.

Several years later I saw Kevin's name on the credits of a very good movie, not in the starring role, but as the director of the movie. I just smiled.

I've had a lot of roles myself, in this business. I spent my entire childhood on a television program, my teen years as a recording artist, my adulthood as the owner and teacher of one of the longest lasting acting schools in the country, and my most interesting role, as a psychotherapist for people in the entertainment industry. And as a result of coaching hundreds of actors, and doing therapy with many actors, musicians, dancers, directors, agents, and others in the industry, I can tell you that to some extent Kevin's story is everyone's story. Crushing defeat, agonizing disappointment, thrilling success, overwhelming passion for the work...this is all part of the business.

Everyday I talk to actors, musicians, and writers who are valiantly working at making their dreams happen. There are very few stories about success simply happening. Instead, most experience a roller coaster ride of thrilling highs and gut-wrenching lows. How do they deal with the frustrations that usually accompany the business? How can they stay centered and focused in the midst of unpredictable employment? How do they stay the course when well-meaning friends and family tell them they'll never make it? For some, being in the business is a lark, a short term adventure. But for others, it is their life. And just like any other artist, performers tell me that doing something else simply isn't an option. They love their work, they love the business, and they intend to remain involved in whatever way they can.

Looking deeply at the emotional aspects of the entertainment industry is what I wanted to write about. This book explores the most common concerns of those of you who like the challenge, and who obviously aren't afraid to take a risk, but who, like Kevin, occasionally wonder how to handle the many challenges.

I think you'll find yourself in some of these pages. My hope is that in addition to finding helpful information, you'll find it comforting to see yourself as part of an artistic community, with much in common with others. All of the questions selected for this book are from people like you who wrote to me. As a contributing writer for the *Drama-Logue* publication, (now called *BackStage West*) I received letters reflecting the issues that are common to those of you in the business.

Whether you're struggling to get that first break or concerned about holding on to your success, you all have one thing in common: similar needs and dreams. To all of you who are striving to make it in the business, **making it** means being given an opportunity to work at your craft, to be respected for your talent, to be financially rewarded for the work you do, and to be recognized and appreciated by your peers and the public.

The purpose of the next thirty one chapters is to help guide you toward these goals.

Chapter 1

PERFORMANCE ANXIETY

Q. Dear Dr. Andrea, I've been an actress for nine years. I've always had to deal with nervousness before a performance, but I thought that with experience I would stop feeling so afraid. Instead, it's getting worse, especially now that I have a major role in a new play. Before each show I'm sick and actually dread going to the theatre.   Dina

A. Performance anxiety is the fear of a shaming experience. And it's universal. From the first grader making her first presentation at school to the Academy Award winner accepting the highest award, fear of being embarrassed or humiliated is experienced by anyone who has the courage to stand in front of a group. And the anxiety intensifies when the audience consists of your peers, or someone you consider particularly important.

Usually, performance anxiety diminishes somewhat when we become confident about our craft and when we're at ease with our surroundings, as when an actor works on a series, sitcom, or soap opera on a regular basis. A theatre production usually causes more anxiety because of the live audience and no opportunity to do a re-take if a mistake is made. Still, after a few nights, performance anxiety is usually reduced to butterflies shortly before the performance begins, and completely vanishes when the actor steps onto the stage.

You're a seasoned actress, yet your anxiety has intensified, which may suggest a problem that many very well known and highly regarded performers experience. If you're wondering whether you can live up to the expectations of those who admire your work and if, because you now have a starring role, you feel the responsibility of keeping the show from closing, you have a whole new set of reasons (in your mind) to anticipate a shaming experience. But you're not alone.

Sir Lawrence Olivier finally gave up the stage for a film career because he felt he couldn't live up to the perfection his audiences expected from him. He felt tortured that he would be harshly criticized by his fans and professionals in the business. In other words, he believed he couldn't live up to his reputation. At least on film he could re-do his scenes if necessary.

Of course, you don't have to give up your theatre career, but you will have to give up distortions in your thinking that are causing you more anxiety than you should have to deal with before a performance.

If, in your idea of your perfect self (we call this the ego-ideal), you believe that you're not worthwhile unless your show is "a hit", the pressure will continue to mount until you diminish your ability to do your best. But if you can change the way you think about it, the importance you attach to it, your anxiety will become manageable.

Of all the different thoughts that seem to crop up before a performance, the most problematic is **catastrophizing**. (I don't think I'll be able to get through this without making a dreadful mistake.) The most helpful thinking is called **realistic appraisal**. (realizing you are bound to make a few little mistakes, but so what?) And "so what" is really the key here.

These could include thoughts like, it isn't essential to receive approval from others in order to have self worth. And, perfection is not required in order to be successful.

Changing your point of view will take effort, because excessive anxiety has become a conditioned response to going on stage. You'll probably find it helpful to do some special mental exercises about 20 minutes before the curtain rises each night. You can accomplish this by closing your eyes, taking a deep breath, and allowing good feelings about yourself to enter your mind. Repeat this night after night, and in time good feelings will appear automatically. Or, you can find a therapist, an expert at visualizations, to help you. Soon your mind will associate going on stage with a feeling of positive regard for yourself.

Remember, Dina, a play is just one tiny element of your life. So put it back into perspective, pat yourself on the back for your courage and for facing your performance anxiety, and above all, enjoy the moment!

Chapter 2

Handling Rejection

Many actors in my practice confide how affected they are by rejection, a common theme in the acting profession.

Q. Dear Dr. Andrea, I've been in L.A. for one year trying to pursue an acting career and I feel like a failure. I've had a number of rejections and lately my agent hasn't been sending me out at all. Sometimes I want to quit the business, but I don't know if I could ever be really happy if I don't make it as an actor.   *Robert*

A. Robert, "success is about going from failure to failure without losing your enthusiasm". I'd like to take credit for that quote, but actually it belongs to Sir Winston Churchill! I've always thought it was a profound idea though, and all successful people have stories about the failures and disappointments they experienced along the way.

Let's face it, no one wants to fail. But failure is a part of succeeding. If you're seeking high goals, you have to be willing to risk failure, many times, in order to reach those goals. Each time you fail, you learn something very important that helps you to get to that next step. Each attempt strengthens your abilities and talents. But, let's take a deeper look at your pursuit and see whether I can help you make the best decision.

First let's examine your goals. We all need to be very realistic about our desires. Whenever anyone tells me he wants to be famous, or become a star, I worry. I believe that this kind of wish (which is very common in our society) stems from the underlying need that we all have: to live a life that is meaningful and memorable. We long to be immortalized, to be thought of as someone who lived an important life. The movie, *Il Postino*, presented a beautiful story about a postal worker whose friendship with a world renowned writer somehow made his life more significant, or at least he thought it did. Of course, fame has nothing to doing with the meaningfulness and importance of our lives. If fame is what you seek, you're wasting precious time pursuing unrealistic and unhealthy goals.

If you told me, however, that you have a passion for acting as a profession and as an art form, and that you would be contented to work at whatever opportunities present themselves, I'd suggest that the one year that you've been trying is not an unreasonable length of time. As you know, this is a tough business, and it often takes years of training and striving to become a respected actor. Whether you're willing or able to devote these years of your life to the pursuit of acting depends a lot on how important it is to you, and whether, perhaps, you have other interests and talents that would be satisfying to you. Of course, if you have a family, your responsibility to provide a stable environment should be a priority. In that case, your involvement in the business will somewhat depend on whether you can actually make a living at it. If you need a regular job, you could still find many avenues to pursue as an actor. But if you're single, and you love the work, then don't let the many rejections you could face discourage you and cause you to quit. Rather, allow the strongest, not the weakest, part of you to determine your future. For example, you might devise a three or four year game plan. During this time you would focus as intently as possible on your interests, doing everything possible to hone your craft, make contacts, and develop your talent. At the end of that time, evaluate your situation. You should know at that point whether you're willing to continue in this profession, or if it's time to discover your true destiny, whatever else it might be.

As you've already experienced, there is so much disappointment involved when you don't get that callback, especially when you know you have talent and did a great audition. But, whether you decide to continue acting, or leave it behind for a new pursuit, to some extent, you will still be confronted with the issue of success and failure. Fear of failure causes some to stop striving, while others accept it as part of life. To change how you respond to failure, begin to reframe failures, mistakes, and rejection as opportunities. Think about all the lessons you learned from a particular failure and create new ways to handle subsequent similar situations. Open your mind to new ideas and opportunities. Don't limit yourself to one goal or one way. Accept criticism and use it to help you grow. Create a full life with friends or family and develop interests beyond your main goal so that it becomes easier to handle failures as they inevitably present themselves. And keep in mind that each attempt you make toward your goal makes you better, stronger, and one step closer to your dream.

Chapter 3

CALLBACKS

Q. Dear Dr. Andrea, Time and time again I blow it at callbacks. I know I have the talent and I get called back a lot, but I disappoint myself and the casting director when I'm called back. I'm my own worst enemy. Can you talk a little about what's going on with me?   *Susan*

A. Many actors aren't as prepared for the callback as they need to be. Perhaps the combination of a lack of preparation, plus the additional pressure a callback creates, results in a less than dynamic performance, causing you to lose the job.

An important fact to remember is callbacks are a numbers game. If three people are called back, you have a one in three chance of winning the role. If they callback 10 actors, you only have one chance in 10, no matter how well you do. All the actors at the callback will be good and presumably very right for the part. As veteran casting director Mike Fenton reminded me, "If you're called back, it's because you're right for the part and have an excellent chance of getting the job. You're there because you did a very strong audition." But, the other nine also did a very strong audition. So having realistic expectations is smart, and will keep you from blaming yourself too much if you aren't chosen. These kinds of disappointments are part of the package you accept when you're an actor. To put it into perspective, you can consider going to auditions as simply part of the job. When you finally land one, hopefully you'll be paid well enough, or it will be a fine showcase for your talent, making the whole process worthwhile. Beyond having a real understanding about the odds of winning the job, there are many things you can do to prepare and increase your chances.

Handling the pressure: The psychological dynamics of the callback are very interesting to me. In most cases actors are more anxious at the callback than they were at the initial audition. The closer they come to winning, the more let down they will feel if they don't. Sometimes there are several callbacks, each one creating more hope, more anticipation, and more fear of losing. Handling pressure is one of the marks of a professional. You have a knot in your stomach? So what? You desperately want this role? Desperation will get in your way. Soften your need to get the job. Focus on the enjoyment of the audition itself. Take pride in the fact that you are part of a small, select group chosen for the callback. Over the years I've seen average actors do a marvelous job under pressure, somehow rising to the occasion and doing better than they ever had before. In reverse, very talented actors, who shut down when it counts, are unable to pull off the strongest performance when it really mattered.

What makes the difference? Confidence, preparation, directability, belief in oneself, an ability to roll with the punches, and handle the unexpected. In addition, a likeable personality and overall experience combine to influence the results.

Preparation: Immediately after your first audition, begin preparing for a possible callback. Make notes about the acting choices you made, your wardrobe, and comments or suggestions made by the casting director. If you get a callback, review your notes and try to duplicate (not improve or change in any way) your first performance. Your goal is to repeat your winning performance, unless the casting director specifically asks for some slightly different approach. Include in your notes some insights into the character you're playing. Include character feelings, motivations, and personal circumstances, which you're likely to forget. You could get a callback in a day or two, or in a month. Much of what was brilliant about your performance may be lost if you don't put it down on paper. When you get called back, begin preparing by reading through your notes. Be certain that you have your lines memorized, or if it's a commercial audition, rehearse at home whatever you will be expected to do. You may have dialogue, or, very possibly, improvisation is required. You'll want to re-create what you did the first time, while somehow making it look fresh and spontaneous. Top athletes are often trained to mentally visualize before a game. This is a proven technique for any kind of performance. Mentally see yourself doing the scene perfectly, with all the appropriate emotion, humor, or intensity. Visualize yourself feeling confident, able to take direction easily, enjoying the whole process, and impressing the casting team.

Flexibility: Planning and preparation are only part of the picture. Many unexpected surprises can occur which you can learn to handle gracefully. The most common frustration I hear from actors is when the other actor, or the reader opposite them, throws a curve. For example, at an improvised commercial audition, you may have a partner who tries to completely overpower you and doesn't allow you to participate in the conversation. With humor and strength, you must address the issue, either by simply interrupting (in character), or by asking the casting director if you can try it again, reminding the other actor that in his enthusiasm he didn't permit you to speak. If you have a passive partner, you will have to take the lead. On the other hand, if you have a very spontaneous partner, be open to a creative, if slightly different approach than you expected. If at a theatrical audition you have a reader who isn't an actor and simply says the lines without feeling and meaning, you're on your own to create mentally what you're not actually getting. Be prepared to be your only source of support. Be ready to shine no matter who reads with you. And if you're fortunate to have good chemistry with your partner—consider it a bonus. If you drop your script, if you lose your place, if you hear a loud and distracting sound, you can incorporate these unexpected events into the scene, with as little distraction as possible, or ignore it, whichever makes sense at the moment. If you hear the casting team talking or answering a phone, or if one leaves the room, refuse to be offended by it and continue. Don't over book your schedule on a callback day. You never know how long you'll need to be there, or in fact, if they may want you to come back again later in the day for a final callback.

Likeability: Because everyone at the callback is at least theoretically right for the role, other things come into play when making the final decision. Likeability isn't talked about much, but when it's down to the wire with more than one great choice, the more likeable actor may get the job. But insincere friendliness is not likeable. Rather, those who have cultivated a professional and considerate manner are easy to direct, remain enthused in a genuine way, and are just simply a pleasure to be around. They have an edge over those with a subtle arrogance, a resistance to suggestions, or a sensitivity to critiquing that makes it difficult to work with them.

Distractions: These are usually from your personal life and can have an enormous effect on your ability to be your best at the callback.

A fight with your spouse, worry over financial problems, discouraging comments from parents or friends can take the life out of you when you most need support. The short term solution is to call up every inner resource you have and prove that you will not be defeated by the outside world. It's a wonderful feeling to know that you are your own strength. In the long run, dealing with your personal problems is very important. You have a right to insist that your family and friends respect your choice to be an actor. If they can't, you'd be wise to not involve them in that part of your life. Financial worries can have a devastating effect on your auditions because you become so needy and lose perspective. Learn to manage these personal problems so they don't creep into the callback and sabotage your efforts.

Susan, you're understandably impatient. All actors have gone through what you're feeling. Relax, take the pressure off, take command at each audition and realize that it's just a matter of time.

Chapter 4

GETTING THE RIGHT AGENT

Q. Dear Dr. Andrea, Can you talk a little about getting an agent? How do I know who's a good agent?   *Debbie*

A. A good agent is the one who sends you out on a lot of auditions that are right for you. Unfortunately, you may not know whether you will become one of that agent's priority actors until you've already signed a contract. You do have a 90 day out clause in your SAG contract, so that if your agent isn't doing anything for you, and you have another opportunity, you can end your contract. There are over 200 SAG franchised agents on each coast, and usually under 10 in the smaller markets. They range from huge full service agencies to small boutique agencies that specialize in one area, or handle a few people across the board. In my opinion, size in no way reflects the quality of an agency. It's all about the people working there and how they feel about you as a talent. Some of the smaller agencies have outstanding reputations for handling talent and building careers.

Everyone dreams of signing with the huge, international agencies like William Morris and ICM, which staff hundreds of agents in every area of entertainment. These agencies have the power (clout) to simply say to a casting director or studio executive, "Look, I'd like you to see my new client for this movie," and more often than not, it is done. Sometimes agents at these offices package complete shows and negotiate multi-million dollar deals which include the on camera talent, the writer, and the director. At ICM, the commercial department only handles celebrities. The William Morris Agency has a commercial department for unknown, newly discovered talent, although most of its clients are semi names, top name talent, and the super stars. The only down side is that it's easy to be forgotten at an agency like this. You could be signed, then literally shelved along with a mountain of other hopefuls. On the other hand, it's very prestigious for a newcomer to be signed by an agency with the stature of William Morris.

You might find between eight and twenty five agents on staff at a medium sized agency, each involved in a specific department. At some of these agencies, only the agent who discovers you has to decide whether to sign you. In other cases, the whole staff meets with you, and they vote on whether to take you on. At an agency like this, you'll have several agents working for you, at least theoretically.

Boutique agencies are small and personal. One or just a few agents handle all the work and represent all the actors signed with them. A few of these small agencies still take on a fairly large number of actors, but most are very selective, signing only those they feel strongly about and for whom they intend to work very hard.

Finding an agent takes perseverance and know-how. You'll need to start out with as much training as possible and a great picture. For a list of SAG franchised agents, pick up a book such as *The Right Agent* or *The Agencies*, and in New York, the *Ross Report*. Begin sending your photo, a cover letter, and resume to 10 agents at a time. Follow up in about 10 days with a phone call and try to make an appointment. Expect to get more rejections than invitations. If you send out 50 pictures, perhaps one or two agencies will be receptive to meeting you, based on how well your picture impresses them and what their needs are at the time. If you're imagining that you'll be able to pick and choose, let me welcome you to the real world. Early on in your career you'll find getting an agent to be very challenging. You may not have several choices and will sign with any agent that shows an interest in you. For commercial agents, you need an interesting, commercial look, an ability to read copy naturally and improv comfortably, and, most of all, a likeable personality. Theatrically, you must have more to offer in order to interest an agent. Theatrical experience, training, or a spectacular look is important.

Although you don't want to skip from agent to agent, realistically, it may take a couple of tries to get the perfect agent. But you need to give an agent enough time to submit your pictures to the casting directors. Even then, if the picture isn't working, you may not get calls. Most of the agents that I've known are extremely hard working. When they believe in an actor, they continue to submit him for auditions even when the actor isn't getting callbacks. If an agency is sending you out regularly, you owe them your loyalty. But it's unrealistic to think that you'll be sent out consistently all year long. Sometimes there just aren't any calls for your type. Over the course of a year there will be very busy months and some slow ones, and you'll wonder if your agent has forgotten about you.

Your relationship with your agent will go through changes too. At first, you may feel hurried or down right brushed off when you call to talk. Just keep in mind that your agent's job is to get breakdowns, talk to casting directors, and negotiate contracts for you. Chatting with you on the phone is a luxury neither of you can afford. Eventually though, as with every long term relationship, you and your agent will begin to see each other as part of a working team. Each helps the other, and a friendship develops based on mutual respect and trust.

You can meet agents by submitting pictures, attending showcases, and through personal referrals. If you have a friend who is signed with a great agent, possibly that friend can get you an appointment. If an agent insists that you take photos with one specific photographer, it may mean that he isn't as interested in you as he is in getting a percentage of what you pay the photographer. If anyone wants money up front, run the other way. SAG franchised agents take 10% of what you earn on a job and no more.

Don't expect your agent to parent you. If you need that, wait until you're successful and get a manager. A good agent is strong and aggressive, can negotiate the best contract for the client, has a good feel for what the casting director needs and senses which actor is really right for the part. Agents who send just anyone to read for a part quickly lose the respect of the casting directors.

If you're in the position of having several agents interested in signing you, during your appointments with them, let them know that other agents have expressed an interest and that you will need a few days to make your decision. That gives you a little time to find out about each agent and the agency. Don't be afraid to use your own gut feeling when you make a decision. If each agency has a good reputation, go with the one who seems most enthused about you. If in a year you discover that you made the wrong decision, you can go back to the other agency and re-establish your relationship.

Chapter 5

STRESS AT THE AUDITION

Q. Dear Dr. Andrea, I'm so upset because at an audition this week the casting director started screaming at me because he thought I wasn't listening to him and then continued to insult me in front of a whole waiting room full of actors. I can handle rejection, but this was really out of line.   *Lee*

A. I've heard this story more than a few times. Part of the problem is that the casting director has a different agenda than does the actor. Although they're both focused on the same project, in some ways they have very different needs regarding it. Casting directors need to be seen by the client as very skilled at finding great talent. They're not primarily concerned with the sensitivities of the actor who very much wants to be the one chosen. The process of casting makes actors vulnerable because they're selling themselves. It's difficult to separate the performer from the performance. You are your craft in some ways. If you sell cars and a customer doesn't like the one you sell, you may be disappointed that you didn't make a sale, but it isn't personal and you realize it. When you audition for a role and you aren't cast, the loss is more personal. It's especially delicate if the actor has been in the business for many years and hasn't been cast for quite a while. Trying to maintain your dignity at a cattle call where a casting director is running late and treats you like a number is difficult. For that reason, casting directors have an obligation to be respectful and professional to every actor who auditions. With a high percentage of actors out of work at any given time, each audition is very important as it represents a potential job. The more the actor needs the job, the more pressure is felt to "land this one". Most of the casting directors that I know are sensitive to this issue and try to put actors at ease so that they can do their best work. It's the wise casting director who creates a comfortable atmosphere in order to pull the best performance out of each actor. It's inexcusable to take advantage of the vulnerability of actors at an audition by treating them as less than equal.

I spoke about this subject with Mike Fenton, one of the top feature film casting directors in the country. At Mike's office, actors are always treated respectfully. During the many years he has been finding talent for motion pictures, he has come to see actors as sensitive, even fragile. He wants actors to understand that at the audition, the casting director is the actor's ally. So if you feel you didn't do your best, you can ask the casting director if you can try again. He wants you to do well. Remember that if you've been invited in, you have already crossed a certain threshold and are considered a strong possibility for that role. Keeping that in mind, plus being as prepared as possible (having the sides learned and character analyzed) can help give you the confidence you need. Then, if you are subjected to an unreasonable casting director, you'll be less affected by it. Mike is very aware that there are some casting directors who treat actors and agents poorly. If the problem is serious enough, a call to SAG might be appropriate.

I also talked to Tom Carnes, an independent casting director (Carnes and Company), about some of the pressures that casting directors face. The "stress of the clock" is one of their most frequent and frustrating concerns. Each project has a deadline. The client expects the casting director to find the right actors quickly. If it's a commercial, there may be two days to cast, and shooting is scheduled for two or three days later. Tom points out that a casting director's job could be on the line if a strong selection of actors isn't available to show the client. And, in fact, a casting director can be replaced in the middle of the job. So try to imagine having to rely on 30 to 100 actors to be dependable, on time, with headshot in hand, and ready to read the copy with a reasonable understanding of the character and storyline. When actors don't show up, are very late, or come in unprepared, it all contributes to a stressful situation. Of course the casting director's individual personality plays into the whole scenario too. Some people are gracious when under pressure and some are not. Some casting directors are abrasive and love the power they have over actors, knowing they have thousands to chose from. Others see themselves and the actors as part of a team, all pulling together to do the best job possible.

Of course I would be missing a very important part of the equation if I didn't ask you to look to yourself to be certain that you aren't part of the problem. Let's examine whether you don't overreact in situations where someone else is in control. Do you magnify the moment, making the injury bigger than it is? Do you provoke negative reactions in others by your arrogance or sense of entitlement? Do you ignore direction, resist suggestions, or in some way disregard the wishes of the casting director? Do you feel insulted or injured when a casting person doesn't acknowledge you, seems not to see you, and hurries you in and out of the audition? Do you understand that the audition process is about finding the right person for the part and is not a social situation where you can expect strokes, compliments, or reassurance, no matter how much you may need them? Are you insincere? Do you flatter and in any way try to ingratiate yourself with the casting director? These questions all point to a subtle narcissism, which, frankly, is common today, especially among actors.

If the problem is with you, it could also suggest a straightforward problem with authority figures. Freud once wrote about the parallels between director as father figure and cast of actors as his children, noting that some children are rebellious and fight the authority of their parents (or director). It is a sign of maturity to accept that, in the context of an acting assignment or at an audition, someone else is running the show.

If you honestly know that you behaved professionally and did not provoke the situation, you can handle it in several different ways. If this is the first bad experience you've had with this casting director, I would give him or her the benefit of the doubt and assume that this is a one time situation. I think everyone deserves to be excused for having a bad day now and then. Simply be as polite as possible and let it go. If, however, there is a repeat at your next audition, do the audition, then call your agent about it and ask not to be submitted to that casting director again. You will probably find that you're not the only person who complained about that casting director. If actors refuse to audition for abusive casting directors, it may require them to rethink their approach. It's very important for you to respond calmly and graciously in all casting situations, partly because you want to protect your own reputation as a professional, and partly because losing your temper can only escalate the situation, causing you to become part of the problem. It's so much smarter to elevate yourself from tasteless, classless behavior.

Each casting director has a style of his or her own. Some are purposely a little tough, but still remain professional, while others are informal and relaxed in order to create a comfortable atmosphere for the actor. Most see the actor as an indispensable part of the casting process. I call these casting directors human beings. The few that do not fall into this category shouldn't be tolerated. Actors and casting directors can do more to understand each other's unique problems and focus their energies on the creative assignment that has brought them together.

Chapter 6

Accessing Emotions

Q. Dear Dr. Andrea, I never had any idea that it would be so hard for me to show emotion. But I've discovered in my acting class that it is very difficult. When I'm given a scene where I need to feel hurt or cry, I just freeze, although I find it easier to show strength, anger or tough-ness. Any suggestions?   *Glen*

A. Accessing your feelings when you need them is developed over time. Of course, when we're little children, we simply cry, scream, fly into a rage, show terror, or express unbridled joy at the moment we feel it. Soon though, we learn that expressing whatever we feel, whenever we please, is inappropriate, and more importantly, makes us very vulnerable to the insensitivity of others. As we mature, we learn to suppress and repress many of our strongest feelings and emotions (as well we should if we want to get along in a civilized world). However, we do pay a price for that suppression, and that price is that some of us lose the ability to feel spontaneously, especially if we know that we're being observed by others. In more extreme cases, some have dulled their ability to feel at all, making it impossible to share intimacy with another person.

I've always believed that one of the reasons actors are held in such high esteem is because they can express the joy, the pain, the torment, the thrill, and the whole range of emotions that we all hold within us, but find few outlets to express. So we weep with the heroine who loses her one and only love, we rage with the action hero when the evil character gets away, we feel suddenly more alive when we watch two lovers embrace. In other words, for at least a little while, we live vicariously, feeling all the intense emotion we must control in our own lives. As you have realized, expressing genuine emotion on the stage or on the screen takes courage and an uninhibited sense of freedom.

For some actors, bringing up the appropriate emotion is as natural as breathing. This type of acting is very visceral and experiential. I call this right brain acting because the right hemisphere of the brain contains our artistic talents. This actor often does extensive and detailed research about the character and scenario, then loses himself or herself in the moment, creating the kind of performance we all admire. But for many actors, spontaneous emotion has to be cultivated. There are many approaches used to tap into our emotions, many of them involving emotional memory and sense memory. You can take classes and read excellent books on these subjects. Remember, though, that acting is not primarily an intellectual process. It doesn't take place in your head, but rather through your senses and in your heart.

What prevents a person from freely expressing feelings? I think it's helpful to understand the nature of our feelings. The better we understand ourselves, the more profoundly we can understand the psychological makeup of the characters we play. Feelings tend to unfold in layers. Often one feeling covers another until the original feeling is so hopelessly buried that we are no longer in touch with it. The layers commonly reveal themselves in the following way: let's suppose that you have just received some terrible news. Your first response might be to have a complete lack of feeling—of any kind. This first response involves denial and repression and serves as a protective defense against the painful feelings that are to come. When you recover from the initial shock, you may feel anger or rage. Anger is usually a reaction and a defense against feeling hurt. Acknowledging the anger and releasing it reveals the hurt underneath. When you are able to express your sadness and voice your hurts, you can get in touch with the underlying fear that caused it. Finally, your fears are often connected to feeling vulnerable and dependent, the way you felt as a child. What you fear most is that your basic needs won't be met. These needs include being nurtured, loved and cared for. In fact, early survival depends on someone willing to provide this care. All of this brings up the need to control yourself and your surroundings in order to be protected from emotional pain. This results in blocking the ability to freely express feelings.

Given the complex nature of our feelings and emotions, it isn't surprising that most of us find it difficult to open up for an audience or a camera. But if you want to act, you need to use those emotions and feelings the way a carpenter uses tools and wood. You can't work without them. One of the best ways to open up emotionally is with a psychodrama group. This type of group combines helping you resolve personal issues that may prevent you from feeling with an opportunity to express all of your feelings in a safe and supportive place.

Another important aspect which often inhibits an actor is a cultural one. Society still places pressure on men (and little boys) to show strength, be tough, not cry. Our culture gives you permission to display these "masculine" qualities and discourages or ridicules softer, more tender feelings. Vulnerability and tears are interpreted as feminine. Women, on the other hand, often struggle in acting (and in life) with the expression of anger, aggressiveness, and strength. Since the 1950's, American society has matured regarding this subject, but cultural norms are slow to change and we still carry with us the harmful gender labels of the past.

Please keep in mind that acting is a craft that takes time and effort. You may have unrealistic expectations and will want to be patient with yourself. Accessing your feelings is one very important part of the whole picture, and also one of the most difficult, but as you continue to study and explore your own personal issues, you will find yourself opening up and freely expressing the emotion needed for each role you play.

One more thought on this subject, Glen. When you are able to bring up your deepest and most powerful feelings, your next task will be to use them creatively as an actor, without allowing unbridled or undisciplined emotion to rule your personal life. It's much smarter to acknowledge and think through the feelings that ebb and flow throughout the day before deciding to act on those feelings. And sometimes it's smarter to just recognize what you feel without acting upon it at all. Fortunately, you are an actor, and you will always have a creative outlet for your deepest and most passionate feelings, which you can share with your audience, who will feel along with you.

Chapter 7

CREATING CHARACTERS WITH DEPTH

Q. Dear Dr. Andrea, I've been told that my acting is "surfacy" and so I'd really like to learn how to create characters with more depth. Another actor said I need to know more about psychology. Do you think this is true? Kevin

A. Some actors have an innate understanding of human feelings and behavior so they can readily tap into their pool of past experiences and emotions to understand the character they will portray. But most actors, especially those new to acting, need to devote some part of their training to studying the deeper and often complicated workings of the psyche. Actors can be seen as "surfacy" for four reasons:

1. They may have very little understanding or experience with the psychological makeup of people.

2. They are still struggling with the ever present problem of performance anxiety, which inhibits their freedom.

3. They may possess very little empathy for others.

4. They may be closed off emotionally (as a protective defense against being hurt) and find it difficult to open up.

In this last case, an actor will find himself conflicted between protecting his own vulnerability and finding the deepest issues of the character. This is why some of our greatest actors admit how much of a struggle it was to become a certain character and live that person's life on the screen. They had to overcome their fear to play the role authentically.

Basically a character is a combination of physical, intellectual, psychological, and emotional qualities. You learn who he is by what the author says about him, what the other characters have to say, and what the character says about himself. Of course, his behavior tells you even more, but it's the actor who turns the character into a living person, bringing uniqueness and individuality to the character. The actor who uses his own psychological dynamics, taps into his own reservoir of emotion, and finds as much in common with the role as possible will have created a character of depth. In fact, even when playing a shallow individual, one that has little understanding of his own actions and behavior, the actor must search for the underlying psychological motivations and, in essence, understand him better than he understands himself. Don't you agree that it will be difficult to do that if you have a limited understanding of human psychology?

So let's begin with the idea of finding commonality between you and your character. Rather than saying "the character does this and feels that", communicate with the director from an "I" approach: "I feel this and I want that." Because in a sense, when you play the character, you become the character, and the character also becomes you. For example, when Robert DeNiro creates a character, parts of his own physical and psychological makeup are woven into the person he plays. As an artist, he selects which aspects of himself he can use to enhance the depth of the character. From a psychological point of view, we can say that there are many facets and personalities within each person. We're not talking multiple personality here! We all have aspects of ourselves that surface in certain situations. Using these different parts of the self to play a role is thrilling. But without insight into all the aspects of your own personal character, it will be difficult to create a stage or film character that possesses the necessary layers which make it interesting.

Sometimes a character doesn't have the depth it should because the actor hasn't put enough thought or effort into developing it. A simple way to create a multi dimensional character is to ask a long list of questions about her. For example:

1. Is she intelligent, or not very bright? Maybe she is clever and cunning. Or perhaps she is naive and too trusting.

2. What about the emotional nature of this person? She may be sensitive or easily hurt, or wildly emotional, easily expressing rage. Perhaps she is fearful or tentative, or full of joy, or spiritually fulfilled.

3. Questions about the psychological nature of a character might be: what are the psychological underpinnings that drive and motivate this person? Is he plagued with insecurities? Does he use defenses such as denial and projection? Is he suspicious and paranoid, or anxious? Is he driven to succeed? Does he find it easy to love another person?

This line of questioning is limitless and will add all the nuances to help you shape the person, from his personality, his manner of speech, or regional dialect, to the way he walks, the tempo of his conversation and any physical limitations with which he may have to deal. And of course, we must not forget the period and culture in which this character lives. A young man and woman sitting on the porch, gazing into each other's eyes and speaking softly, will be entirely different if the script puts this scene in a small Mid-Western town in 1920, rather than Manhattan, 2010.

Finally, acting that is representational, that is, choosing to indicate the emotion rather than really feeling the emotion, is the result of superficial analyzation of the script and character and inability or unwillingness to dig deep into your own psychological nature. You are your best source of understanding and inspiration. You have the ability to create a character in a way that no one else can.

Chapter 8
CREATING STRUCTURE

Q. Dear Dr. Andrea, I moved to LA from New York and was successful right away, landing a play and signing with an agent for commercials and theatrical. Now, several months later, I'm not working and the agent has sent me out three times in five months. I have a pattern of going full throttle, gaining some success, and then I burn out. Sometimes I can't sleep at night and then I fall asleep in the morning, and sleep half the day. I do come up with lots of ideas, but when I wake up, I go into a big black vacuum that sucks the life out of me. I waste a lot of time watching TV because I'm not very disciplined. S

A. **Control, focus, structure, and self discipline**. These are the concepts that I first thought about when I read your letter. Your letter was a reflection of the state of your life, touching on many issues, but lacking focus. It suggested that these four elements may be lacking and are causing you to become sleepless and depressed.

Control: In a study done in the 80's, it was shown that individuals who have a strong sense of self efficacy (that is, a belief that they have reasonable control over their lives) were usually capable of coping with all of life's events and were reasonably contented. Those with little self efficacy (little control over personal and professional aspects of life) became hopeless and weary. These studies, done both with animals and humans, produced the same results. When individuals felt unable to have some control over events, they lost hope.

If I had to name a serious occupational hazard for those who don't go to regular, daily jobs, it would be the negative effects of a lack of structure, focus, and control. Some people handle lack of structure well, because they function at a higher level when they're not bound by strict schedules and prefer flexibility of their time. Or they're self disciplined and provide their own structure, rising at the same time each day, planning specific activities for the week, and adhering to a routine which gives them boundaries. This helps ground them in an otherwise unpredictable world. When you're trying to become successful in an unpredictable profession, look for other areas of life where you can maintain some measure of control. You should find an interest where you needn't rely on others to succeed.

One aspect of becoming an actor that isn't talked about much, but which I consider crucial, is to understand your mental strengths and weaknesses and your personality type. It takes a certain kind of temperament to handle the daily uncertainty that actors face. You seem to blame yourself for the fact that your agent isn't sending you out and that you're not employed. It's typical for a person who is feeling little self efficacy to blame yourself rather than attribute the problem to the nature of the business. Or maybe you don't really understand that being out of work and not getting calls from your agent are typical, even if you're a self starter. The bottom line here is that you may not be suited to the vagaries of the business. If this is the case, it's unproductive to blame yourself. Frankly, I would hate living with daily uncertainty, and so would many others. But before you think that I'm telling you to find another life goal, let's see if I can give you some tools that will help you be happy while pursuing an acting career. Conquering these could be useful whatever turn your life takes.

Focus: A lack of focus is a sure way to let your life slip through your fingers. Focusing on a few, small projects is better than overwhelming yourself with large, unrealistic ones. One step leads to the next. Focusing on small steps gives you small successes along the way. Focus should never be solely professional. It should be divided into personal and professional. That way, if one isn't progressing, you'll have the other to keep you feeling balanced. Keep your focus on tangible, productive projects which enhance your life. Refuse to be unnecessarily distracted.

Structure: Set your alarm fairly early, for the same time each day. Allow yourself to lie in bed for ten minutes and then get up. Have a place to go at least four mornings a week. Join a gym, take up a sport, or take college classes or workshops on a regular basis. Find a part time job which will give your week predictability. Do something for someone else every week. Help an elderly person in your neighborhood; volunteer to help with troubled children or teens. Take some steps toward your career every week—at the same time of day if possible. Write down every one of those great ideas that come to you and make steps to implement them. Make a daily list every morning and try to accomplish everything on your list by the end of the day. Plan something social every weekend. Since you're fairly new to LA, you may be feeling somewhat isolated. It takes time to build friendships in a new city, but friendships will add structure to your life. Belonging gives our lives meaning. Regular meetings with a theatre group, sports club, or anything else that really interests you will serve the purpose of helping you find friends and increase your responsibilities toward others. Eat meals at the same time each day and go to bed at about the same time each night. In other words, you're creating structure in your life where none exists. All of this requires self discipline.

Self Discipline: This one separates "the men from the boys." It requires you to delay gratification and work at something even when you want to quit. When you have self discipline, you refuse to give in to that inner voice that pulls you down and weakens you. It's what motivates you to continue even when you're discouraged. We don't become self disciplined by reading about it or because someone tells us we should be. It's always self taught, difficult to achieve, and very rewarding when we've done it. It's a mind set, an inner determination, helped along by focus and structure. Because you're not sleeping, you may be depressed. There may be a deeper cause beyond the frustrations of the acting business, and so I think you should find a good therapist to talk to. Treating the depression may change your whole outlook.

Once you're free from depression and seeing things clearly again, you can honestly evaluate whether you're temperamentally suited to the ups and downs of being an actress. If you're not, don't fight your basic nature. When you force yourself to be what you're not, you're taking precious time and energy away from finding and pursuing your true purpose. If you feel that you can continue acting, be prepared for uncertainty and compensate for that uncertainty by adding control, focus, structure, and self discipline to other areas of your life.

Chapter 9

STRIVING FOR THE IMAGE:
EATING DISORDERS

I received several letters from actors and actresses with eating disorders. The pressure to be thin touches almost everyone who wants to work in front of the camera. Actresses and models are willing to play with their health in order to live up to social and cultural demands. I hope that the following letter and my response are helpful to you and anyone else who is struggling with these frightening disorders.

Q. *Dear Dr. Andrea, I am a model and actress and I'm starving myself. I'm hungry all the time, yet, I won't allow myself to eat. I feel sick so much of the time and on my last modeling shoot, I was very weak. No one seemed to notice. I've tried to work this out by myself because I feel as though my career is at stake, but I can't seem to pull myself out of it. I've lost a lot of weight, but I still feel fat. What can I do?* Joan

A. Joan, There's a lot more at stake here than your career. You could lose your life. You need to get help now because anorexia, which is what you've described, cannot be ignored. You need to enlist the help of a family member or a good friend. You also need the help of a hospital, a psychiatrist, or an eating disorders clinic. The more support you get right now, the better your chances for a complete recovery. I'll list several referrals at the end of this chapter.

It amazes me how many people in the television and film industry have been touched in some way by the pressure to be thin. Of course models and actors, whose images we see, and whose perfection we demand, feel the most intense pressure. Yet, eating disorders like anorexia nervosa, bulimia nervosa, and binge eating are found among people all over the country, in many different professions and social groups. The most serious of the eating disorders is anorexia, an all consuming, life-threatening illness that has been extremely difficult to treat. Fortunately, professionals in the psychiatric field have begun to better understand the underlying dynamics and possible genetic links of the illness and have developed new ways of treating it.

The symptoms of anorexia include refusing to maintain a normal body weight, intense fear of becoming fat even though you are underweight, a distorted body image, that is, feeling fat and seeing yourself fat, even when you're undernourished and underweight, and in women, the absence of regular menstrual cycles. Extreme weight loss is accomplished by a severe reduction in food intake along with intense exercise. Most people with this disorder deny or minimize the severity of their illness and are resistant to treatment. Often by the time family or friends step in to help, serious damage may have been done. Hypothermia, hypotension, edema, bradycardia, kidney and liver failure, and, tragically, death can result from lack of treatment. If you binge and purge, you may also have a related disorder, bulimia nervosa. Often, a person will be anorexic for several months and then switch to bulimic behavior, which allows her to eat. The two most noteworthy behaviors associated with bulimia are secret, planned eating binges which include thousands of calories consumed, followed by purging through vomiting, diuretics, or laxatives. Most bulimics talk of bingeing as their greatest source of pleasure and comfort, yet they feel as though the binges are out of their control. After an episode of bingeing, they feel an overwhelming sense of self-hate and depression, which leads to the next secret binge, and the cycle continues. In addition to these two serious eating disorders, countless others binge, then fast, in a struggle to get the nourishment they need while desperately trying to strive for a thinness that may be unrealistic.

Eating disorders are caused by a complicated interplay of elements. These include the value our culture places on thinness at any price, dependence on external validation, a need for control, a desire to please, and an intense pursuit of perfection in oneself. When perfection isn't achieved, the person often feels unworthy. And according to the most recent research, there is probably a neurological or biochemical predisposition to the illness which hopefully, in the near future, will be corrected with proper medication. Add to this mix of circumstances a severe stressor such as a move to a new city, the death of a family member or the break up of a romance, and anorexia or bulimia may be set in motion. For when one cannot control the outcome of circumstances in the world, at least she can control her body (and be admired for it). Carolyn Costin, MFT, who specializes in the treatment of eating disorders at the Eating Disorders Center of California and is a successfully recovered anorexic herself, told me that effective treatment must concentrate on several important elements. These include individual and group therapy, plus nutritional and medical supervision. In some cases, a stay at an in-patient treatment center or a hospital, and medication, along with constant monitoring may be needed. Ms. Costin's approach focuses on the "healthy self" versus the "eating disordered self", as though these are separate aspects of the person which require integration, much the same way treatment of multiple personality focuses on integration of the personalities. This approach seems useful to me since those with eating disorders often speak of a force beyond their control (the disordered self) causing them to starve or binge. The Rader Institute at Washington Medical Center Hospital in Los Angeles, the Monte Nido Treatment Center and UCLA also have in-patient care for these disorders. If you live outside Southern California, you can find treatment centers in most major cities, or you can call the National Association of Anorexia Nervosa Associated Disorders (ANAD) at 847-831-3438 for information. If you have absolutely no funds, you may be eligible for Medicare/Medicaid, or occasionally a hospital will treat those in need.

I'd like to recommend two books. In *The Secret Language of Eating Disorders*, by Peggy Claude-Pierre, the author writes that eating disorders develop in people who are so concerned about the feelings and opinions of others that they fail to learn to love themselves. Unconditional love is an integral part of her therapy approach. The second book, *It's Not Your Fault*, by Russell Marx, MD. explains the complicated mixture of cultural and family influences, combined with neurological and chemical malfunctioning, that creates eating disorders.

How much are you willing to sacrifice for your career? Now is the time to focus on your health. When you've successfully freed yourself of your eating disorder, you may find that you can still have a modeling and acting career, and be healthy and energetic enough to sustain it. One of the biggest fears that you may have is that once you start to eat again, you won't be able to control how much you eat or how much weight you'll gain. With proper treatment you will once again learn what each of us is born with, the body's ability to know how much it needs. You'll learn to listen to that inner voice and to respect it by eating according to your own inner wisdom.

Whatever it takes, Joan, keep searching for the care that you need right now. You can recover.

Chapter 10

COSMETIC SURGERY

Q. Dear Dr. Andrea, I'm a 40 year old actress and both my agent and boyfriend think I should consider a face lift. I don't know what to do.
Barbara

A. Having cosmetic surgery is so personal a decision that I cringe at the thought of you allowing anyone to influence you in either direction. But I can explore the issue from as many directions as possible in order to help you make the best decision possible.

The desire to emulate the beautiful images we see in the movies, on television, and on the pages of glossy magazines, is, I believe, the number one factor in making cosmetic surgery so significant in our culture. In the early 50's we looked up to those special people on television, in a very innocent and naive way. Gradually, though, I have seen a change in the attitudes of ordinary people. We're asking: why not me? We believe we can be every bit as beautiful as those we see on the screen, with a little (or a lot) of help from cosmetic surgeons. The perfect faces that never seem to age gave us the idea that if the stars can do it, we can too. Although cosmetic surgery is popular in other parts of the world, nowhere is it as widely used as here in the United States. It is so typically American to take action, to solve problems, and to have the attitude that anything is possible. We don't have to live vicariously by watching those we admire on TV. We can be on TV, (if we are willing to bare our soul for a TV talk show). We can be beautiful. We can be significant. We can be admired—and remembered, and loved. Isn't this what it's all about? As an actress, particularly if you do films, you feel the pressure of your fans, who insist that you remain young and beautiful. As long as you can remain ageless, perhaps they can too.

During World War I surgeons repaired the faces of disfigured soldiers, giving them new faces and a brighter future. At the end of the war, some doctors began a marketing campaign through the media targeting the general public (especially women and people with "ethnic" features) about the miracle of cosmetic surgery. Other doctors were horrified at the idea of doing surgery simply to change a feature that was disliked by the patient. Unless the patient was in the theatre or TV and movies, these doctors refused, saying the person was not a good candidate for surgery and needed therapy instead!

But the public rejected that point of view and demanded procedures for themselves that had been reserved for celebrities and the very wealthy. Doctors and patients (mostly women) created the phenomenon of cosmetic surgery for the simple purpose of improving one's looks. In a book called *Venus Envy*, Elizabeth Haiken points out that the stigma of narcissism that was once attached to cosmetic surgery has largely vanished and in its place is the concept that improving one's appearance is a valid and useful pursuit. Some people want plastic surgery because they feel it will give them more personal power. A nicer looking face or body can make you feel better about yourself, giving you the confidence to try new things, reach for higher goals. Whether better looks actually help you find a better mate or make you more eligible for a promotion is questionable. I know plenty of people with less than beautiful faces who have outstanding careers and loving mates! But if you're in front of the cameras, there is no doubt that cosmetic surgery is an option that you will consider, because nowhere is someone more scrutinized than on the screen. Still, you don't want to be swept away by the Hollywood pressure and the popular impression that doing a little "nip and tuck" can be decided upon casually. For one thing, you need to consider your image as an actress. If you're a character type, you might be much better off allowing the years to make your face more interesting. Not all actors and actresses opt for surgery. But if your career has been based primarily on your looks, you will be motivated to explore the idea.

From a feminist perspective, the individual who improves her appearance through cosmetic surgery may achieve some kind of personal power, at the expense of women in general. In a college dissertation on cosmetic surgery, the writer complained that women have always had to go to extra lengths, even risking their health with surgical procedures, major surgery and all the risks associated with anesthesia, in order to look like a young, Anglo Saxon American. If you were middle aged, had an Italian nose, had Asian eyes, or...well you see where this is going...you needed to correct the problem. This attitude outraged the author, for she believed that each woman who participated in cosmetic surgery procedures exacerbated the problem for all other women, perhaps gaining personal power, but weakening the cause of women and minorities overall.

A more contemporary point of view on the subject (and my own personal one), looks at cosmetic surgery much the same way I look at all modern medical technology. There are exciting procedures which improve people's looks (and at least theoretically their lives) and there are serious risks that tend to be downplayed by practically everyone, including doctors and the media. This is why it's extremely important to make your own decision, without the influence of your agent and boyfriend. Your decision should be based on as much information as you can gather. Women in their 20's, especially those who want larger breasts, are particularly vulnerable because their youth and inexperience have not yet prepared them for the possibility of complications.

However, complications do occur, as they can in any type of surgery, so you must be very careful when choosing your doctor. Most candidates for plastic surgery don't realize that anyone who has a medical degree can be called a specialist and obtain a license that permits him or her to practice any type of medicine, including cosmetic surgery. To protect yourself from inexperienced and unqualified doctors, be certain that the person you choose is certified, and, preferably, a diplomate of the American Board of Plastic Surgery, or a member of the American Board of Medical Specialties or American Board of Facial Plastic Surgery. Be certain that your surgeon is experienced in the procedure you need. Ten years experience with face lifts does not qualify someone in breast augmentation or liposuction. Educate yourself before making an appointment so that you can ask intelligent questions when you have your consultation. An excellent book, *The Plastic Surgery Source Book*, by Kimberly Henry, MD. and Penny Heckaman, will give you information about most of the major surgeries and the cogent questions you will need answered by any doctor whom you consult. Of course one of the best ways to find the right surgeon is through a personal referral. If you know someone who has had beautiful work done and who had an overall good experience, I would consult with that surgeon.

In my practice, I've worked with people who've had different types of cosmetic surgery. Some surgeries have been very successful. Some had complications or bad results, while others came through it with ease, looking beautiful and natural.

Barbara, don't allow your agent, boyfriend, or anyone else to pressure you. Think this through on your own and make the decision that is in your best interest, not only for your career, but for you personally.

Chapter 11

JEALOUS PARTNERS

Q. Dear Dr. Andrea, My husband and I are actors. We've both had some impressive successes and also some long periods of time when we were out of work. We've always been a little competitive; still we were happy, even when things were bad. But now, I'm on a series, making more money and getting more acclaim than I ever dreamed possible, and I honestly think my husband is going to leave me. He says he doesn't know how he feels about me anymore because I've changed. I'm so upset I can hardly concentrate on my work.

No name

A. Envy and jealousy have many masquerades. Men especially don't want to appear needy or dependent and so are more likely than women to become angry or, as in your case, indifferent, when they start to experience jealous feelings. Competition in marriage drives a destructive wedge between the partners. Instead of combining their talents, intelligence, and love to create a safe haven against a tough world, fear spurs one or both to take the "every man for himself" approach. This is what your husband is doing. And it isn't uncommon. Jealousy is just one of several reasons why many show business marriages don't survive. There are so many circumstances that can cause insecurity and jealousy between the partners, and these circumstances are more frequent and in many ways more intensified in the business. The person who is prone to jealousy has a very difficult road to walk.

But we can't ignore the fact that lovers betray each other. How can we trust, when our culture looks the other way as important people and celebrities cheat, when our "role models" obviously don't value honesty, when devotion isn't even considered a value to be admired? This unfortunate fact of our culture makes some inclined to trust even less. We do a lot in our lives to avoid reliving the earliest hurts from childhood. We construct an outward persona, a mask that hides who we really are. This often begins so early in childhood, that even we don't know who we really are. This mask usually shows the outside world a confident, secure person. Your husband wants to maintain his mask by not admitting to you that he feels threatened and fearful of your success. Choices are made (often unconsciously) to safely avoid ever reexperiencing the devastating emotions which now have been successfully buried. These defenses work well as long as we don't allow others into our inner world. Most of us, though, are healthy enough to want attachment to someone, and we're drawn to and driven to intimacy with a special person. But the closeness that we so passionately need requires us to put down that mask, leaving us as vulnerable as we were as children. Jealousy is one of the mechanisms by which we try to control our circumstances and avoid the devastation we anticipate.

Your husband is both jealous and envious of you. His jealousy arises out of the fear that his inability to match your success will lead you to lose respect for him and search for someone new. In a sense he wants to abandon you before you abandon him. But he's also envious of your new position. He sees others admire you the way he wishes to be admired. He wants it for himself and is selfish enough to want to destroy the satisfaction that you deserve to enjoy now. The issue of who has the power in the relationship comes into play here. It may be very important for him to hold the power in the relationship, so that he can continue to feel secure. Your new status may make him anxious and resentful. He may leave as a way of punishing you for becoming more successful than he and thus destroying his grandiosity. As he compares himself with you, he feels diminished. Rather than seeing your success as his success, he sees a gain for you as a loss for him.

Your husband can overcome his feelings of envy and jealousy. My sense is that he is completely out of touch with how overwhelmed he is by the way your lives have changed since the success of your series. The high profile wife, the money you bring to the marriage, the change in the balance of the relationship have probably made his own position in the world look painfully lacking. You may be able to bring the whole issue out into the open and help him realize how much you love and need him. It's too bad your husband doesn't understand that a TV series is not the most important criterion determining the value of a man. If he realized this, he would be able to participate in your success and enjoy it for the pleasure that it gives you. If you and he could have that deepest and most intimate of conversations, speaking the unspeakable, admitting your deepest fears (for I am sure that you have some fears of your own), he may realize that he doesn't want to lose you and that your marriage is really worth saving. Ironically, marriages can be put to the test during bad times and good times! I think the finest role models for a great show business marriage were Jessica Tandy and Hume Cronyn. They somehow overcame all the ups and downs of the acting profession—together. They were respected by their fans and those who knew them personally. I always admired that marriage because I saw them as two people with the same vision. They pursued their dreams together. They understood that the business is too unpredictable to require both people in the marriage to reach the same level of stardom. A strong marriage will endure whatever comes along.

You and your husband can turn this situation around. Assure him that you are at his side for all of his ups and downs, and you need him to be there for all of yours. And in the midst of your personal struggle, I hope you'll remember that this is your moment. You have the right to relish it and to expect your husband to support you.

Chapter 12

COMING OUT

Q. Dear Dr. Andrea, What's your opinion about coming out? I'm 20 and gay and I'd really like to be honest, especially with my parents, but I'm afraid of how they will react and how it will affect my acting career.   *Dean*

A. Our sexuality is a totally private matter. I believe that all sexuality is best expressed within the context of a monogamous and loving relationship. Promiscuity, whether gay or straight, is immoral, dangerous (in light of the AIDS virus), and soul killing. And because it's a personal and private matter, I think coming out should depend on the personal circumstances of the gay or lesbian person. In a perfect world, we could all be just who we are without the negative and unfair consequences that many homosexuals have had to endure. Ideally, you should be able to tell your family and close friends without fear of abandonment. Parents who disown their homosexual children are ignorant and unloving. Those who can't rely on family to accept them will hopefully create a family of friends who do. Whether or not you come out in other aspects of your life, especially in your career, is a decision that should be well thought out. Some express tremendous relief when they've been open about their sexuality, because the stress of living with a secret was just too high a price to pay. Being open is liberating. For some, secrets are humiliating. It means hiding your life, your friends, your partner—in fact it means hiding everything you are. For others, privacy is a right they intend not to relinquish. Who can tell them that one way is the only way? I certainly wouldn't presume to.

However, I think we must draw a distinction between who we are and what we do. From what science now tells us, it looks as though homosexuality may be neurobiological in nature. Beyond that, though, we're totally responsible for our behavior. I think some who disapprove of the gay lifestyle assume that all gays have careless and casual sex. And before the devastating effects of the AIDS virus, many (but certainly not all) did live that lifestyle. AIDS has matured the gay community, helping it to evolve into a more monogamous group, with different values and a high level of responsibility.

Over the centuries people have dealt with the issue of homosexuality with many varied attitudes. I'd like to believe that people are expanding their attitudes to include an understanding and acceptance of the nature of homosexuality. In the Middle Ages homosexual behavior was considered a sin, but the person was not considered abnormal. In the sixteenth century homosexuality was considered a crime and a sin. Later, in the nineteenth century, modern medicine, and particularly psychiatry, viewed it as a mental illness, spending the next fifty years trying to find a causal relationship between homosexuality and key environmental factors—like overbearing mothers or passive, unavailable fathers. As a result, a very creative and ultimately useless array of treatments was offered, from intense psychoanalysis to partial lobotomy. In 1948 Kinsey (the famous sex researcher) attempted to find patients who had been converted from homosexuality to heterosexuality during these various treatments. He could not find one patient whose sexual orientation had been changed. It was possible, in a few cases, to decrease sexual behavior, but not desire. Psychiatry consistently failed to show that homosexuality was simply a preference and a lifestyle choice which could be reversed. And, it failed to show that it was pathological. As a result, in 1973, the American Psychiatric Association removed homosexuality from its diagnostic manual, recognizing that it was not a disorder that needed treatment.

In 1991, a study was done which concluded that a part of the brain, the hypothalamus, was different in male heterosexuals and homosexuals. Putting this into perspective, we realize that much more neurological study has to be done before we have the complete picture. Eventually, a biological basis for homosexuality will probably be discovered, but cultural and environmental factors also have an influence.

Flaunting homosexuality is probably a reaction and resistance to being forced to hide who you are and a lifetime of being unaccepted.

But it isn't smart or dignified to do so. There are ways to express sexuality which bring us satisfaction without making a public statement. I don't believe that same sex marriages diminish the sanctity of marriage. Rather, it offers gays and lesbians the opportunity to make the same lifetime commitment made by heterosexuals. However, I feel that children should be raised by a mother and a father and are better off in a home with opposite sex parents, because children benefit from the differences each sex offers.

At the LA Gay and Lesbian Center in Hollywood, Media Relations Manager, Corri Planck, told me that having a well thought out plan is important before coming out. From one's family, there are many different responses ranging from total acceptance to total rejection. Many parents react somewhere in the middle, with some disappointment, some guilt, a lot of ambivalence, and mostly with a lack of understanding about the nature of homosexuality. Many believe that it's simply a personal choice or preference; others believe they've done something to create your homosexuality; others have the reaction, "We've known for years; what took you so long to tell us?" Because you may not know the response you'll get, prepare by being as self sufficient financially as possible, and surround yourself with others who can support you emotionally. If your parents need help adjusting, you can suggest they call PFLAG, (Parents, Family, and Friends of Lesbians and Gays). This organization has chapters in most major cities and offers support groups that help to educate families and encourage family closeness and understanding.

Your approach toward the rest of the world depends on what kind of work you do and whether it's safe to reveal your homosexuality. In the military and in other circumstances where homophobia is common, it's not wise to come out. Where losing your job or fearing for your safety is concerned, coming out is a luxury you can't afford.

In the entertainment industry the decision is complicated. On one hand if you don't come out, you must be prepared to hide your life, your partner, your past from the spotlight—no easy task. The more successful you become, the more relentlessly the press will dig to learn about you. On the other hand, are your fans ready to accept you as a leading man if you're openly gay? Will coming out affect your career? These are tough questions, but realistic ones, that you need to face.

Dean, I'm looking forward to a world where people are accepted for their differences. Sometimes I get discouraged because I see so clearly how the ignorance of some can cause so much pain to others.

I know you've been hurt by the self righteousness of people who must find someone to reject. Just live your life and make your decisions based on your own particular set of circumstances. We really are on the brink of acceptance and understanding that homosexuality is not a moral, ethical, or religious issue, but a biological one.

Chapter 13

Losing the Dream Job

Q. Dear Dr. Andrea, After three callbacks, meetings with the director, and signing papers to keep me available for a starring role on a dramatic TV series, I was cast in one of the major roles. I'm an unusual type and great parts are hard to find, so I was absolutely thrilled. I believed I could be a star. It really was the happiest time of my life.

But after the first season my agent told me that I was going to be replaced. The only reason given is that the show was going in another direction. Well, I am devastated about it. I'm so down I can barely get out of bed. I just don't want to see anyone and I know I'm pathetic. I wanted to prove to my parents that I could be successful. I need help.

G.D.

A. G.D., you've come face to face with the realities of the business. You're feeling this level of disappointment precisely because you held your dream right in the palm of your hand, and never did it ever enter your mind that it would be taken away from you. Life throws us these curves and we all must learn to handle crushing disappointments in a way that will ultimately strengthen us, rather than destroy us. You're in the throes of a reactive depression. This type of depression is brought on by an environmental factor that pulls the rug out from under you, leaving you temporarily without a feeling of stability and predictability in your world.

A profound sense of loss is the overwhelming feeling during a reactive depression. The loss can be real (losing a great role) and symbolic (feeling that this was your chance to prove to your parents that you could be a success). And this sense of loss leaves you feeling certain that you'll never be able to fill the empty space that it's left in your life.

Typically, reactive depression is caused by loss of a loved one (through death or a broken romance), a job, an opportunity (especially if it's perceived as a chance of a lifetime), social status, or by moving away from home and loved ones. How one overcomes this type of depression depends very much on his or her psychological make up before the loss occurred. Some consciously acknowledge the disappointment and the pain, and quickly take steps to replace the loss with new pursuits. Others spend years carrying a low-grade depression (called dysthymia) which allows them to function, but without much pleasure. On some level they believe that life can never be as good again.

There are some things you can do to move yourself quickly through this. First of all, rely on your family or closest friends to help you now. You need to talk to someone who will be a good listener and understand the depth of your disappointment. However, once you've expressed your hurt feelings, distract yourself. Go out, find a new interest, take classes, spend time with people, and just generally get your mind off your loss. Push yourself, even though you may prefer to stay at home alone. The less active you become, the worse you'll feel. Secondly, this is a great time to read the inspiring biographies of some people you admire. You'll be amazed at the adversity and disappointment almost everyone has to endure to reach the highest levels in his profession—the movie business or otherwise. How many years did Dustin Hoffman pound the pavement before he found the perfect role? How long did John Travolta wait before his career exploded the second time around? Most actors can tell you wrenching stories of discouragement before the big break came. Thirdly, realize that if you came as close as you did to the prize, you must have talent. If you had it then, you still have it. And unless you were dropped because you were difficult to work with, it's fruitless to ruminate over why the program producers or network higher-ups made the decision they did. The sooner you shake this depression, the sooner you'll be ready for the next opportunity. Finally, change your focus from becoming a television star to being the finest actor you can be. The movie star fantasy, the super star dream, keeps you from being realistic and may be the source of your anguish. The wrong handling of these painful situations often leads to drug use, destroyed relationships, and heart-break, especially in young performers who can't handle the pressure.

Work on your craft and on emotional and psychological balance. When the next movie vehicle presents itself, (or in fact, any kind of opportunity) you'll be more prepared for it in every way.

But, G.D., if your symptoms continue, please find a good therapist. The type of depression you're experiencing usually doesn't require medication, but responds well to time spent looking introspectively and acquiring insight about yourself. Remember that destructive coping, such as escape through alcohol or drugs, could destroy your chances for the future you dream of. Good therapy is an excellent coping mechanism which will give you tools to get through this and prepare you for all of life's surprises.

Chapter 14

Holiday Blues

Several people wrote to me about holiday sadness, but one letter seemed to capture the essence of what many people feel during the holiday season. Changing the way we think, we can look forward to the holidays with as much anticipation as we did when we were children.

Q. Dear Dr. Andrea, I'm always a little down at this time of year, but this year in particular I just want to avoid the whole thing. My career has been one disappointment after another and I broke up with my boyfriend last summer. I can't even afford to go home to see my parents. How can I make Christmas bearable? *Tina*

A. Ask a few people how they feel during the holidays and at least you'll find you have company. Others struggle with the same issues you do, often because we set up an ideal holiday in our minds, and anything that falls short of that ideal is rejected as a "bad" holiday. Holiday depression has one thing going for it...it's temporary! Even so, closing your eyes to the holiday season is next to impossible, and deprives you of a very nice experience—even if you can't be with your family or create the perfect holiday scenario. Loneliness is one cause of holiday sadness. You may actually be alone or you may be surrounded by lots of people—the wrong people—who accentuate your feeling of loneliness. When we're fortunate enough to be with someone we really love and who really loves us, the holidays are a time to anticipate. What we do at Christmas is a reflection of what we've done throughout the year. If you haven't reached out to others or spent time wisely working toward a worthwhile goal, you may have regrets.

At the year's end we also tend to review our accomplishments and disappointments. One more year passed, one year older, and we assess whether we've come any closer to our plan...to act, direct, compose, or publish our music or screenplay. Or in our personal lives, did we find a fulfilling relationship. Especially in this business, dreams don't always come true in exactly the way we envisioned. Sometimes even the attainment of all our goals brings about new problems that can leave us disillusioned. And at the end of the year, as we look back, we feel disappointed. This kind of thinking leads nowhere, and requires firmly changing our perspective to visualize what we do have and what we have accomplished. We can reframe literally every event that occurred over the year and turn it into a useful experience from which we can learn something valuable for the future.

Long held guilt or anger tends to surface at this time of year too: guilt over people we may have hurt, ways in which we may have been dishonest with someone who trusts us, or even misguided guilt for leaving home to pursue a career, leaving loved ones behind. Anger that we continue to carry or grudges that we insist on keeping alive serve to turn inward upon us and cause unhappiness. Christmas and Hanukkah are meant to be symbols of love, gratitude, generosity, spirituality, and peace. As our society drifts further and further from these meanings of the holidays, they are replaced with rushed schedules, frantic buying, overindulgence, and a sense of simply enduring the chaos. Rather than "endure", I think we can find ways to enjoy—even treasure this time of year, every minute of it, for whatever it is. I believe that the secret is living in the moment (all year long, but especially now) and appreciating each day for what it is. This is a difficult concept for people to grasp, because, we're so indoctrinated to the contrary, thinking in the past and in the future— but rarely in the very moment that is now. We ruminate about yesterday and tomorrow, allowing the preciousness of the present to slip right through our fingers. Think about how many days, weeks, or even years we may have lived without really noticing the present moment. When you live in the present moment, you're practicing mindfulness, an Eastern philosophical concept that has become appreciated by many here in the United States, especially Southern California. In fact, I've known several talented actors who practice mindfulness when creating a role, and we're all familiar with the admonishment of acting coaches who encourage you to be more real by being "in the moment".

Let's abandon our single ideal of the perfect holiday. Instead, Christmas and Hanukkah can be acknowledged by small gestures of kindness and thoughtfulness to a few people—maybe one person. We don't have to create the fantasies we see on television or the holiday we remember from childhood. Let's appreciate the little moments, the one Christmas carol instead of the constant noise, the sip of cider rather than the huge feast, the small but meaningful gift instead of the extravagant one. If you feel an emptiness in your heart, reach out to someone.

And what a relief it will be. What a beautiful way to escape the stress of unrealistic expectations. Quiet the mind, reject all the hype, do a good deed, and refuse to be distracted from what the holidays truly symbolize.

Chapter 15

SERIOUS DEPRESSION

Q Dear Dr. Andrea, I've owned my own talent agency for 14 years. Frankly, I never thought I'd write to anyone about a problem, but I seem unable to solve mine anymore. As a child actor I was abused by my manager. I had some therapy and got on with my life. Now I feel I'm going nowhere. I'm divorced, my children are grown, and my job is a constant struggle. I can't stand the business anymore, I can't sleep and am totally exhausted. I've felt this low a couple of times in my life, but this time I can't shake it.   *HB*

A. HB, you're describing a mood disorder, specifically a depressive disorder, with many different underlying causes and some very effective treatments. I'll cover the different types of depression, but whichever symptoms seem most like those you're enduring, you need to get some help. Major depression includes depressed mood, possibly combined with lack of interest or pleasure in almost everything, fatigue, feeling worthless or guilty, having difficulty thinking or concentrating, insomnia or hypersomnia, loss of appetite or binge eating, feelings of hopelessness, and recurrent thoughts about death, almost every day for at least two weeks. It becomes almost impossible to function during an episode of major depression and requires immediate attention by a psychiatric MD, because we're always concerned about the possibility of suicide. Dysthymia is more of a low level, chronic low mood, which is diagnosed if it lasts at least two years. Actually, some people have been dysthymic since childhood and are so accustomed to the way they feel that they move through life, functioning at a certain level, but never actually feeling good. Manic depression is a bipolar disorder involving wide swings in mood, from manic, causing wild, sometimes dangerous behavior and risk taking, to a crash so low that depression is like a blanket covering the body, mind, and soul.

Some also experience depression following surgery, childbirth, menopause, a traumatic event, mental or physical fatigue, or extended stress. Depression can also be brought on by certain drugs, (prescription or illegal-recreational), infections and viruses, brain chemical imbalances, and depletion of certain hormones. Reactive depression is a reaction to life circumstances, like the loss of someone you love, or a major disappointment. And, anger turned inward, that is, anger that has not been acknowledged, somehow expressed, or resolved is another cause of depression. In many cases, and very possibly in yours, there are several causes for depression. First, there are many more cases caused by chemical disturbances than is realized. Our brains and our bodies are producing dopamine, serotonin, amino acids, endorphins, and many other natural chemicals, keeping a very intricate balance in order for us to stay healthy. These chemicals and hormones, which tend to fluctuate, have an affect on our minds, and in reverse, the thoughts and emotions that flow through our minds can profoundly affect our chemical balance. Our physical and mental being is intricately interwoven, making it illogical to separate the two when trying to diagnose depression.

So, I would first recommend that you see a psychiatrist who can properly analyze your particular set of symptoms. Short term use of certain anti-depressants might be a good beginning. Some doctors are treating mild cases of depression with amino acids and have reported a very high success rate.

Secondly, you need to get back into therapy. You sound like the kind of person who "toughs it out" rather than allowing others to help you. Childhood abuse and exploitation take a toll, and although you've done a good job overcoming the pain of your childhood, I think that you're ready to begin a new phase of life. It may be time to deal with the real fury that you feel toward your childhood manager and your parents who somehow were unable to protect you from the peril in which you were placed. In addition to therapy specializing in childhood abuse, I would soon follow that therapy with a cognitive *thinking* type of therapy, which I believe is the most important key to permanently avoiding further depression. In this last phase of therapy you'll look at how you miss being needed by your children, plus reassess your job as a talent agent, exploring options for your future. This will give you the opportunity to make some very important decisions about the way you want to live the rest of your life. The lifting of depression will help you change the way you think about your life's events and give you the courage and energy to make new choices. Once you've corrected any chemical aspect of your depressive disorder and faced your anger about the abuse, changing the way you think becomes the most crucial component in avoiding another episode of depression.

I know that depression slows you down and depletes your energy, but you must make that first step and get help. Depression is circular in that the less you do, the less you are able to do and the more depressed you become. Make yourself find treatment, which includes therapy that specializes in childhood abuse, follow this with cognitive therapy to help you map out your future, a psychiatric work-up that may include medication, and add outside activities that bring you pleasure. Wellness is also circular. The more you do, the more you will want to do, and depression will fade in time.

Chapter 16
Go Ahead, Make a Change

If making a major life change is so exciting, why does it cause so much anxiety? Because, every change, even a wonderful one, also involves some loss.

Q. Dear Dr. Andrea, I just accepted a contract part on a soap opera. Financially, I will earn more money than I've ever earned in my life, and it's a great role. This should be the happiest time of my career, but there's a big problem. The show is produced in New York! I've never even been to New York, and now my family and I are going to live there! And what if the show is canceled. We're leaving in two weeks, the whole family has mixed feelings and I can't sleep. How do people deal with this kind of thing?   *Robert*

A. Congratulations on your new job and your new life in New York. The questions and doubts that you're wrestling with are a normal part of any major change that we make in our lives, but the worry and anxiety that accompany change often make us doubt our decisions and cause us to want to retreat to the comfort of what we know and to what we are accustomed.

First let's look at what your greatest fears may be. You mentioned that maybe you'd make the big move only to find that the show has been canceled. Well, I suppose it could happen, but I think it's widely agreed that daytime drama is a relatively stable area of the television industry. It's very possible that the show you're joining has been on the air for many years. In fact, the longest running television programs in the country are the soaps.

Maybe the deeper question is whether you worry that you might be canceled. Your contract may stipulate that your story line can be dropped before your contract is up, leaving you without a job. I know it's difficult to leave everything behind when there's even the slightest doubt about the permanence of the job. Unfortunately, in this business, uncertainty is the norm. I do think, though, that you have reason to feel fairly secure about your future on the show in New York because of the extensive auditioning that must have been done to find you.

As you know, auditions were probably held in New York first. When the appropriate actor for the role wasn't found there, the production team found it necessary to start looking on the West Coast. Once in LA, I'm certain that they saw many actors. When you're having doubts about yourself, remember that the search was conducted on the both coasts and they selected you.

Still, it's always a good idea to be realistic about the future and perhaps wait to sell your house here in LA, if that's at all possible, in case you find it necessary to come back, or if in fact after your contract is up, you and your family long to return to Southern California.

If you have children, you're probably wondering what impact a move will make on them. A popular opinion among some "experts" in the field of child development is that decisions about when and where to move should be curtailed because children's lives shouldn't be disrupted. I don't agree with this view.

In many cases children benefit from living in different places and meeting new people. These children become resilient and adapt to change gracefully, attributes which are extremely valuable later in life. Moving to new places offers children the opportunity to widen their world, and by meeting new and interesting people, they develop social skills that will be useful for the rest of their lives. Children find security in being with their parents, wherever their parents desire to go.

There are some exceptions to moving children. For example, a teen's senior year in high school, when graduating with his or her class is a very important life event. Every effort should be made to consider the special times in each family member's life and find creative ways to deal with those situations.

A major change will create some ambiguous feelings for everyone in your family and ambiguity creates anxiety. Our ambiguity stems from a deep understanding within all of us that change involves some loss.

Even when we're eager to begin a new and exciting life, we must say goodbye to what we had. We've become comfortable with our surroundings, our habits, our attitudes, and our usual activities. If we choose to make a major change, a part of us is excited about the possibilities and another part is afraid, or at least wary of what the future holds. It's important to recognize that loss is a part of life. By accepting this idea, we learn to accept change as a normal part of life.

Change is healthy. We all need to stretch occasionally, both physically and mentally. Resistance to any change is stifling and unrealistic because everyone encounters circumstances in life where change is unavoidable. Your attitude toward changes will determine how well you will adapt to the challenge these changes present.

This is a good time to reframe your sleepless nights as a reflection of your excitement rather than your fear, and help your family see this episode in your lives as a rare and wonderful opportunity.

Chapter 17

BORDERLINE

Q. Dear Dr. Andrea, I'm in love with an actress (I'm also her agent) and the relationship has been like a roller coaster ride. For over a year I've been trying to understand her, hoping that she'll settle down. But she's very unpredictable. One minute she can't live without me and the next, she wants space. In public she's overly sexy and tries to create attention to herself, sometimes embarrassing me. She has used drugs and drinks too much, but I'm fascinated by her and can't seem to let go. Beyond our crazy personal relationship, she has caused some trouble on a set, by repeatedly not showing up on time, and it makes me look bad to others in the business. She's beautiful and talented, but a director told me she's trouble. Still, she can be very loving and I know she cares about me . I love her and want to be with her, in spite of it all, and so much want to help her. Richard

A. If you decide to stay, be prepared for a wild ride, because what you're describing in your girlfriend sounds like a personality disorder called **borderline**. People with this personality constellation are very impulsive, unstable, intense, unreliable in their interpersonal and professional relationships, have a lot of difficulty being alone, sometimes physically hurt themselves (like cutting themselves to feel alive), and have chronic feelings of emptiness and boredom. Some professionals have said that Marilyn Monroe may have had this personality disorder, creating chaos and causing commotion for everyone in her life. Your girlfriend probably needs and seeks constant stimulation. She may move from drugs to alcohol to sexual acting out, possibly even gambling, in an attempt to stimulate herself. The hardest part for you is undoubtedly the fact that she vacillates widely in her need and desire for you, from intense dependency to an insistence on space and separation when she feels that you're getting too close. This is not to say that she's incapable of having a permanent relationship. A stable, loving relationship does seem to have a calming effect on people who have borderline features, as it would for anyone. I worked with a woman like your girlfriend for several years. In spite of her erratic behavior, I was very fond of her and found her to have many very endearing qualities. She was surprisingly easy to love. At one point a very stable and patient man came into her life, offering her love and consistency. They married, and in some strange way, complemented each other. He was orderly and serious, and she was spontaneous, fun, and free spirited. They each brought something to the marriage that did not exist within the other. I won't kid you, it wasn't easy. He accepted the fact that life would be one crisis after another, and it was.

Please don't think that your love will be able to cure her disorder or change the aspects of her personality that you find difficult. Accept her as she is or leave the relationship, because most of these characteristics may reduce in intensity when circumstances are good, but won't disappear entirely. One common aspect of this personality is a frantic attempt to avoid real or imagined abandonment. Some theorize that abandonment early in life (real or symbolic) has created the disorder, during the phase of life when toddlers are first attempting a bit of independence from mother, who has separation issues of her own. Others believe it's the fault of a biological or chemical difference. Because of an intense desire to be loved and avoid abandonment, people with this disorder are often attracted to high profile professions, like acting, seeking mass approval and unconditional admiration and love. But the harsh realities of the business, (bad reviews, rejection, and shows closing or going off the air) throw them into a state of crisis, bringing up the abandonment issues that always lie beneath the surface. That's when wild acting out with substances or other self damaging impulses (including possible suicide attempts) can come into play.

As you know, her relationships are all or nothing; anything that is not total love can turn to hate. Anything less than total commitment is considered rejection. You're either idealized or devalued—sometimes all in one day! She's unable to regulate her emotions in the same way that you are and may have relatives with the same disorder. Many have been, in some ways, abused or neglected as children. Masterson, an eminent expert on development, contended that the borderline's dilemma is a conflict between desire for autonomy and a fear of parental abandonment.

You know, it's very common for therapists to cavalierly advise people to break up with their current partner for practically every fault. Lack of communication skills? Get rid of her. Not ambitious and hard working? Lose him. I don't agree with that, especially when you're dealing with faults and weaknesses that all of us have. And I'm not going to tell you to walk away from this woman, even though her problems are serious. Only you can make that decision. Only you know whether you have the tolerance, understanding, and love to handle a lifetime with this kind of problem. Go into it with your eyes wide open, with realistic expectations about who she is and who she may always be. This choice has to come from the healthiest part of you, not the neediest.

In order to do that, you'll need to have a clear understanding of your own psychological dynamics. Focus on your own motives and deeper issues. If you have a pattern of being drawn to a wounded woman, is it because you feel stronger and healthier when you compare yourself to her? If so, is that fair to her? What if she improves and gains personal strength and psychological well-being? Will you love her less? Will you encourage her to get better? And will you accept her whether she does or doesn't? Some men who are attracted to this kind of woman are narcissistic or compulsive. These personality configurations are drawn to borderlines like bears to honey. The unpredictability of life with this kind of person is a magnet for some people. It can be sexually exciting and challenging, but is not a solid base for a good relationship. Examine your attraction to her. Analyze her less and yourself more.

If you choose to, there are several things you can do to help her, all of them having to do with creating stability, trust and boundaries in her life. She can improve with the help of long-term, psychodynamic psychotherapy which also includes practical day-to-day help. You must encourage her to stay in therapy when she has the impulse to quit. If she was abused as a child, special therapy is required first. There may be times when medication will be appropriate. If she drinks and uses drugs during difficult times, you will insist that she participate in a 12 step program. Your own devotion to her will be a model she can emulate and you will require that she be monogamous. If she isn't, you should leave. You can create consistency and structure in her life and offer her enduring love. But, Richard, you must also receive enough of what you need from her to make it work. If she is capable of loving you, in spite of her enduring pattern of behavior, the two of you may succeed. I wish you both well.

Chapter 18
THE BIG DECISION

One of the questions that I've been asked is "How long should I keep trying to pursue an acting career?" I know that this topic is on the minds of a lot of you because the answer will shape your future. It's definitely a life changing question. So for Karen, Karl, Anne, Rick, and everyone else who's pondering this decision, here are my thoughts:

In some ways this question is equivalent to asking how long should I stay at one slot machine. Although no one can predict what's around the corner, you can learn to become a good decision maker. Good decision making comes with self confidence and self esteem. It requires that you be as honest and realistic about yourself as possible. Always make decisions based on your strengths, not just your fantasies and wishes.

There are two avenues to take with respect to pursuing a career as an actor. Both are good, solid approaches, but only you can decide which works better for you. Some people go into this business with a time frame and time limit in mind. This person might have a five year plan in which every effort would be made: extensive training, theatre experience, networking, showcasing, finding a good agent, and generally gaining as much experience as possible, to become a working actor. If you take this approach, at the end of that five years you assess, by asking yourself whether you are where you want to be, or even close to that goal. This is a good approach for those who have other interests and talents and who need to begin acting on other choices while there are still viable alternatives. I personally have always seen life as a huge buffet with lots of interesting choices to sample, with one selection more interesting than the next. Acting is but one delicious selection among many. If this philosophy resonates with you, then the "time limited" approach is the one you will inevitably choose, as some interesting opportunity will come along and away you will go!

The second approach is the "in it for life" plan. A person choosing this approach will stay the course through good times and bad. This makes sense for several circumstances: you have a life long passion for acting that can't be replaced in any other way; you have a good job in some other area of the entertainment industry where you can use your position to your advantage; you have a good job in another field which gives you enough financial security and flexibility to allow you to pursue acting; you're contented to view acting as your avocation, or you're retired and can pursue acting as a second career.

If one of these applies to you, then you may want to continue to work at it—forever. With this plan you have a better chance of eventually succeeding because you're in it for as long as it takes. This kind of life is very interesting because continuing to pursue acting is exciting and creative and makes the more mundane aspects of life tolerable. Don't you agree that you can more cheerfully do what's necessary when you have other pursuits that bring you happiness? The only down side to this plan is that you may never achieve great success in any profession. That's the chance you take. I've seen actors spend their lives wondering when the big break will come, waiting tables, hoping this year will be better than the last. Each part that comes their way is the encouragement they need to try a little longer. If they had devoted those years to another pursuit, they'd likely be successful at it by now, making a good living, feeling the confidence that comes with achieving. But...and here's the rub. Only you can know whether you would look back and say I gave it my best shot and I'm glad I pursued other avenues, or whether you would be filled with regret for having walked away from the world of acting.

An effective way to approach a decision is to make a list of very specific and probing questions. By the time you've searched your soul in the answering of these questions, you should have your decision. Here are a few questions you might want to start with:

How strong is your desire?

How talented are you?

How well can you handle rejection?

How much effort have you actually put into the pursuit?

How much training have you had?

How long have you been trying?

What level of success have you actually attained?

What kind of feedback have you received from others in the industry about your chances?

What other talents do you possess in other areas that may be ignored and left undeveloped by focusing only upon acting?

To what extent will an acting career affect your personal and family life and are you willing to make personal sacrifices for it?

You are the best person to assess whether you have a realistic goal or just a fantasy. *You* are the only person who can count the personal cost of pursuing that goal. *You* know whether the quest is making you happy or unhappy. And, (now here's the tricky one) only *you* know whether you honestly want this and have a least some possibility of having it, or whether you have a pattern of striving for the unattainable because it distracts you from a deep source of pain in your life.

Focusing on the unreachable, whether it be a career, an unavailable love object, or a material possession, is a form of fantasy that helps divert our attention from feelings of hopelessness. If this is you, coming to terms with your underlying sadness will be the key to making decisions based on solid, healthy motivation. You want to walk that delicate balance between desire and practicality, because you need to be well grounded in reality to make good decisions. It's the ones who dare to dream and dream big, combining those dreams with their most intelligent thinking and diligent work, that find themselves holding the prize.

One more thought on the subject: there aren't many decisions you make in life that can't be reversed. Who says you can't change your mind? With that shift in consciousness from rigid to fluid, you can make the decision that seems best right now, and, later if you wish to, turn in another direction.

Chapter 19

DEALING WITH ANGER

Q. Dear Dr. Andrea, My boyfriend completely lost it during the rehearsal of a play he's directing. Two of the actors walked out. Unless he can change, I'm leaving him too. When he gets angry he shouts, throws things and threatens. He's never really hurt me or anyone, but the name calling really gets me down. Is there anything I can do to help him change?   *Name withheld*

A. Your boyfriend's anger habit will be as difficult to break as any other kind of compulsive behavior. But he's got a lot to lose and, hopefully, that will motivate him to change. There are so many types of anger and so many reasons for it that it will be helpful for him to understand the underlying dynamics. Understanding, though, is less important than his own personal resolve not to accept this aspect of his personality. Losing you and ruining his reputation in the business might be enough to force him to do some honest self reflection. Frequent and out of control anger is a habit that becomes automatic, compulsive, and feels normal to the person doing it. It has been built upon thousands of past repetitions, beginning in childhood. When he gets the results he wants, the behavior is reinforced, encouraging him to do it again. I like the book, *Letting Go of Anger*, by Ron and Pat Potter-Efron. They point out that each of us has an anger style, a way of being when we feel angry. Anger is a natural part of the spectrum of human emotions. But anger is difficult to handle and can cause a lot of problems in our lives. Some people mask their anger. They may avoid feeling and expressing anger at all costs. Anger is then expressed indirectly, or at the wrong person, in the wrong way. Avoiding anger when it's reasonable to be angry really takes a toll on your well being. It leaves you feeling powerless and often results in physical illness and depression. In fact, the cause of one type of depression is anger turned toward oneself.

Others have explosive anger styles. They shout, swear, intimidate, throw things, and get their way through bullying people. This is shame-based anger and is the result of feeling terrible about yourself. Shame is a belief that you are inherently bad or defective. Beliefs like "I am worthless" or "nobody loves me" are the centerpiece of the shame-based person's identity and can result in explosive and angry behavior. Shame and rage are connected in the following way. Since it takes a lot of courage and a long time to face shame and resolve the painful issues that cause it, many people cover their shame with defenses like arrogance, perfectionism, or anger. This is a unique type of anger called narcissistic rage, an extremely powerful anger that gets triggered whenever the person feels attacked, disregarded, or disrespected. Anything that is interpreted as criticism is seen as an attack on a glass-fragile sense of self worth.

Anyone who coaches actors is aware of the over-sensitivity that some have being critiqued, as if the critiquing is the deadly enemy to a faltering sense of self. Shame bound people will then frequently fly into a rage to protect themselves. Behind the rage is the thought, "I'll make you feel like dirt because that's what you think of me. Don't get too close so that you can see my shame." Shame fuels this kind of anger, the anger drives people away, and the person feels more shameful and lonely. If anger is shame-based, you can change by realizing that the rage episodes are connected to how shameful you feel. Begin to heal with a good therapist and always, always treat others with the respect you want for yourself.

Deliberate anger is a fake display of rage used to get a result. There are four reasons why people purposely work themselves up into a rage: to make others do what they want, to show off, to keep others at a distance, or to avoid real feelings and maintain emotional control. First and foremost, though, is that anger is a manipulative tool to gain power. Gaining power through fear is the way some survive in angry families and dangerous neighborhoods. It's about survival at its most basic level and certainly not about living well or living smart. You can say goodbye to deliberate anger because you want to move to a higher level of consciousness and because the cost of deliberately getting angry is too high.

Cases like these are common, where vicious, angry attacks result in lost jobs and relationships. If your boyfriend engages in deliberate anger, he may have a difficult time giving up the power he has over others. I can assure you, though, that there are other more effective ways to get what you need in the world. Intimidation is a very primitive, very base manuever that eventually causes resentment and defiance in those around you.

Addictive anger results when a person gets hooked on the excitment of a fight. Some couples stay connected by their anger, keeping the relationship alive through emotionally chaotic fights. Some actually seek out situations that will anger them because they're drawn to the anger rush. Anger rush is a strong physical sensation that comes with getting furious. Anger activates the body, giving it an adrenaline boost. The brain becomes flooded with rage and you feel a heightened sense of energy that can be as hard to give up as a drug. If your boyfriend is easily bored and looks for reasons to get angry, he may be addicted to the high he gets from it. Addictive anger is dangerous because, as with all addictions, the intensity must continually be increased in order to get the same rush. Gradually the fights get bigger and more out of control, and the results can be tragic.

Habitual anger is less dramatic, but every bit as chronic. Thousands of people walk around feeling angry from morning until night. Some people are always grumpy, grumbling, and fussing about everything. Others are on edge, allowing every small event to spring them into action. They focus on small injustices and annoyances, blow them out of proportion, and use them as an excuse to express their indignation. Instead of getting what they need in life by thoughtful negotiation, they alienate others and create more reasons to be angry. The questions that need to be asked are these: Is the angry person willing to examine his pattern and take responsiblilty for it? Is he willing to change? Is he willing to take every step necessary to replace anger with other more appropriate behavior? Can he abandon the anger rush? Will he learn to recognize the triggers that set him off and intercede with new behavior that will calm him? These new patterns can be learned by studying the book I've recommended or by finding a therapist who is experienced in dealing with anger issues. Your boyfriend may think that flying into a rage is part of being a strong director. He's actually showing immaturity and demonstrating that he doesn't have the skills to get what he needs from the actors. But the respect that he'll lose in that arena is less important than what he'll lose in his personal life. If you decide to leave, he will come face to face with the harshest consequence of uncontrolled anger, loss of love.

Chapter 20

SUPER STAR FATHER

Q. Dear Dr. Andrea, My father is a super star. No matter what I accomplish in my life it seems worthless compared to his accomplishments. He is loved and admired by everyone—except his family. He cheats on my mother and barely knows his kids. I can't tell you how many years I tried to win his attention and love. I was ignored by him and now I realize that he doesn't love anyone but himself. My question is this: I've been offered a book deal for his story. I'd like people to know the truth about him, but my brother is trying to talk me out of it. It would be the sweetest revenge.   Jack

A. A book deal? I can think of much better ways to resolve the anger you carry and the anguish deep within you. A tell-all book is the choice a lot of bitter, angry, or opportunistic people make, and so often everyone is diminished in the process, but no one quite so profoundly as the writer. It's important to understand the ramifications of an act like this, when the bottom line motive is revenge. I can think of more than one child of a famous person who wrote an uncomplimentary book and displayed the family misery on talk show after talk show in order to sell more books. These books are often fueled by feelings of being misunderstood and by a powerful need to grab some of the attention and public sympathy that has been bestowed on the famous parent. The child of a star can easily feel overlooked, even invisible. It's doubly difficult when that star's public persona is completely different from the private one. The family must endure the darker side of a celebrity's personality, often including neglect of children or betrayal of the spouse. The awards, fame, admiration, money, and glamour that swirl around him or her overshadows what the family knows to be true, which is that this super star is very human, and in many ways is not the hero the public wants to believe he is. It takes a strong person to live in the shadow of a super star, especially when that super star is really an ugly human being.

There are four typical ways of coping with this problem of living in the shadow of a famous parent. You can become an underachiever, hopelessly overwhelmed at the thought of living up to your father's achievements. The dynamics behind this approach is that you can always say you never tried because it wasn't important to you. This way you avoid failure. The second approach is to use his celebrity and your private relationship with him to make a name for yourself, as in writing a book about him. This looks like a great solution to the unfairness of it all. He was a bad father and still gets accolades while you and your family suffered throughout your lives and sacrificed without any appreciation. A book could make you famous and possibly wealthy. What you trade for those perks is that you continue to be negatively connected to him, which doesn't give you the freedom to break free and become your own person. When you write a scathing book about a famous father, you become simply the bitter child of a famous person. Who wants that? The third way is to become outrageously rebellious, embarrassing your celebrity parent, thus hurting him the way he hurt you. The fourth approach, and the really healthy one, is to become a separate adult, with your own talents and goals, your own family and your own mission in life. A worthwhile mission in life, one that enhances your self respect and makes the world a better place, is a far more impressive life choice than being a movie star. And if you don't believe that, you have a lot of maturing to do. You could actually use your famous name to head up an important cause, shine light on a terrible injustice or start your own worthwhile project. You could use that name to attract the press for a meaningful pursuit. Or you could choose not to use the famous name at all, making your own way, with integrity and self respect.

Although your problem is complicated by the fact that your father is famous, the deeper issue is really the "father wound" that he has caused by betraying your mother and neglecting you. An absent father sets up a profound hunger for fathering. This can be conscious or unconscious. It has probably affected the most central aspects of your life. You might have a powerful fear of abandonment and a lack of basic trust. You may be very dependent on others or may show the world a pseudo-independence, yet lack a solid base of real confidence and self-direction. A distant father withholds the encouragement and attention that children crave. He may be emotionally distant, a workaholic, or he may never have bonded to his children. If he's too invested in his own interests to the exclusion of theirs, children remain underdeveloped and ill equipped to handle quality personal involvements. If you weren't valued and loved for who you were, you grew up without some of the key nurturing ingredients that result in a mature and healthy adult. By confronting the anger, the hurt, and the sadness his lack of involvement caused, you can transform your life, making up for what you didn't get.

In the book, *Where Were You When I Needed You Dad?*, by Jane Myers Drew, Ph.D., she suggests some steps to healing:

1. Increase your awareness of Dad's impact, defining what you missed with your father when you were young.

2. Mourn and express the anger and hurt you feel, through therapy, diary writing, painting, or other avenues of expression.

3. Reappraise your father by looking at him as a human being, with weaknesses and limitations. Work toward forgiving him and letting go of any expectations that he might change.

4. Become your own good father, by making loving connections with others. Allow someone else to be like a father to you and learn to become a good father yourself.

5. Acknowledge that the hurt you've experienced can make you a more empathetic person and a more loving mate and father.

6. Possibly you can reconnect with your dad once you see him in a new light. If that can never happen, let him go.

A close and loving relationship with your mother should help compensate for what is missing with your father. Too often we spend our energies pursuing a parent who ignores us, while barely noticing the one who has always shown love and devotion.

Once you've worked through all of the levels of feeling you've carried for so many years, you may be able to find something positive about him that you can focus upon. Did he ever give you his time, his advice, or his support (even if only financial)? Doesn't his position in life offer you some unique opportunities? Try to remember how he may have had a positive influence on you in some way. See how his own upbringing and the limitations of his parents may have influenced him. Focus on a kind gesture or a thoughtful word of praise. We all have to surrender our idealistic vision of our parents and replace it with a more realistic picture of who they really are. Once we have accepted their limitations and acknowledged our own, we may find that we can have some kind of relationship, not an ideal one, but one that is valuable.

Jack, you can follow the path of several celebrity children, spending hours of your time and all of your most creative energies writing a book that keeps you stuck in the pain of it all. You can allow the media to use you, colluding with them to sensationalize your personal loss for their own gain. And for a little while you may fool yourself into believing that you have a tiny slice of your father's celebrity, while at the same time showing the world who he really is. But if you're wise enough to sort all of this out privately, you won't look back 20 years from now regretting the words you put onto those pages, words that cannot be erased. Instead you'll have the satisfaction of knowing that you never gave the tabloids an opportunity to put their own spin on your story. You saw the value in rising above those who will do anything to be on a talk show or interviewed by the press. You won't live in the shadow of a celebrity father. You can be your own man.

Chapter 21

SHADOW SYNDROMES: AUTISM AND ARTISTIC GENIUS

Q. Dear Dr. Andrea, My son is a brilliant composer and pianist, but sometimes he seems like he's in another world. He doesn't date because others see him as strange. I always thought that he was just eccentric, but his personal manager suggested that I should get him some help because when he is forced from his work routine in any way, he becomes upset. When he was very young I left him for four months to tour with a musical and I wonder whether I've harmed him.   *Candace*

A. One of the best books I've read this year, *Shadow Syndromes*, by Ratey and Johnson may have the answers you're looking for. This book fills a big gap in the psychological diagnostic manual that is currently used by most professionals in the field of psychology and psychiatry. Ratey and Johnson have finally put a name to those subtle, but certain personality types that can't really be called mentally disordered, yet they are distinctly different from the average person. Therapists often work with people who do not have a mental illness or a specified psychiatric disorder, but who instead seem to have a subtle version of a well known disorder—a shadow syndrome. I think this book helps us to understand that every person has a brain which functions differently. Every brain is going to have its unique problems, which from the outside will look like emotional or cognitive deficits. Our brains develop according to our individual genetics and change and adapt in response to our experiences. Traumatic events can change our "gray matter," but our biology creates a predisposition to one syndrome over another. There are at least six different shadow syndromes discussed in Ratey and Johnson's book. Your son seems to show some mild signs of autism, which Ratey calls autistic echoes.

As with most people who show subtle signs of autism, your son's strengths and talents lie in his work, and his deficits are seen in his social world. He is unable to cultivate social skills that the rest of us find second nature. He probably has difficulty communicating and articulating his ideas and most likely finds it next to impossible to make casual conversation. But he composes and plays the piano the way very few of us can ever hope to. In both mild and full blown autism, social difficulties are the defining trait, along with a physical awkwardness and lack of ease or grace. However, Candace, when the traits are mild, these people are usually able to marry, have families and work—especially work.

Your son has difficulty when he's taken away from his usual routine because work offers him structure and predictability, which soothe and quiet the internal noise he may be experiencing. Actually, all the shadow syndromes, (mild obsessive-compulsive disorder, mild depression, mild attention deficit disorder, intermittent rage disorder, and mild hypomania), are responsive to routine, schedules, and structure. Many every-day people who live with these syndromes flourish in a stable work environment.

It's a good idea to get help for your son, but not necessarily psychological help. Especially when dealing with a shadow syndrome, the simple life choices one makes matter tremendously. Your son may need more sleep than you do, and according to recent studies, a walking exercise program can affect the brain by sharpening the memory, speeding up response time, elevating mood, and increasing self esteem. Researchers found significant improvement in the behavior of even severely autistic teenagers following aerobic conditioning. Of course, your son's music is his greatest nourishment and will provide him with purpose and meaning throughout his life.

One other concept that Ratey discusses which will be useful to you in helping your son is dealing with anxiety in his life. You can help him avoid what is called the "tipping point" in a given situation. We all have circumstances in our daily life that tip us toward or away from anxiousness. Too many stressful and unhappy situations can cause your son to "tip down", causing his autistic symptoms and behavior to intensify and create distress. When life is on an even keel and stress is kept to a minimum, it is called "tipping up" and we feel peaceful and harmonious. All of us, with and without shadow syndromes, must learn how to avoid too many situations which will create stress and negativity in our lives, so that we don't reach our tipping point. However, some are able to handle more complicated lives than others. Those with shadow syndromes should know and understand their limitations. Your son can learn to be responsible for how much change and stress his brain can handle and choose to avoid his tipping point. You might want to mention this to his personal manager if he tries to push your son beyond his capabilities.

As to your concerns about leaving your son when he was very young, I would be the first to agree that leaving a child for a long period of time is a very big mistake. Nothing is as crucial to a child's development of basic trust as the consistent presence of loving parents. No doubt he suffered from that separation. However, autism is neurological in nature and is not caused by problems in parenting. You might find it helpful to join a group which deals with the aspects of living with someone like your son. Guilt and frustration are common among people who care for the slightly and intensely autistic child and it will be comforting to talk with others who can understand. And, Candace, I hope you've carved out a life for yourself. Your son seems to be a highly functioning, very mildly autistic who could and should develop some independence. I hope you have interests and friends separate from him.

Finally, the very mildly autistic have a lot to offer the world—just as they are. They see the details, the parts, as opposed to the whole. It would weaken the human race if we all thought and observed the world the same way. We wouldn't have some of our greatest works of art, music, or inventions were it not for those who have a deficit in one area of the brain's functioning—and genius in another.

Chapter 22

DYSLEXIA AND ITS EFFECT
ON YOUR CAREER

Q. Dear Dr. Andrea, I'm 18 and have dyslexia. I know I have talent and have been able to hide my problem from my agent and at auditions by picking up the sides early and memorizing really fast. But yesterday at an audition they handed me a completely different piece of copy and when I tried, it was a disaster. I left crying. Maybe I should quit acting, right?   *Marlene*

A. The only obstacle you face as an actress with dyslexia is with cold reading. I'm certain that cold reading technique is difficult for you, and probably always will be. But this kind of obstacle should by no means deter you from acting, especially if you have a natural gift for it. Maybe you're willing to quit so easily because you're still hurt by a history of embarrassment as a result of dyslexia.

When we think of dyslexia, we usually envision a child struggling to keep up in school. Children with dyslexia become adults with dyslexia. Yet the reality is that dyslexic adults fare no better or worse than the general population after high school. Countless people with dyslexia have become enormously successful, in part because they came to terms with their disorder and because they were highly motivated to overcome the disadvantage with which they were born. As with so many examples in life, "what we think, we become". The dyslexic who perceives herself as having an insurmountable burden will be unable to overcome obstacles, while another will develop into a person with great drive and perseverance, accustomed to fighting and winning against all odds. Some of the success stories are extraordinary, considering that the average person with dyslexia reads, writes and spells at a 4th grade level. Yet some of the great names in history— Winston Churchill, Leonardo de Vinci, and Albert Einstein, who was named Man of the Century by *Time Magazine*—weren't defeated by their struggle with dyslexia, although their problems were compounded by the fact that no explanation had been given for their problem. Instead they were labeled as stupid or slow and hopelessly doomed to a very limited life.

Of course we live in a much different world now, where written language is communicated quickly through computers, fax machines, E-mail, and the Internet. And books teaching us how to grasp the new technology are on the market by the thousands. First graders are learning on school computers. And it amazes me that in the midst of all of this, there are still no solutions to the problem of dyslexia. Why do we still have people who cannot adequately read, write, and spell? Well, partly it's because like you, people tend to try to hide the problem rather than seek help for it. According to Kathleen Nosek, author of *Dyslexia in Adults*, the answer lies in the secrecy associated with dyslexia. It is the hidden disability. The typical dyslexic has average or above average intelligence, leads a normal life, may have many accomplishments, and still manages to hide her difficulties with reading. Her dyslexia is a source of shame. A lifetime of cover up often results in behavior that eventually takes its toll on her and her family. And the dyslexic is an expert at faking her way through all kinds of situations, starting with experiences at school. Actually, many children slip through school misdiagnosed, facing each miserable day in the classroom, living for the day that school is behind them, if they don't quit first.

There are three groups of people and three ways they handle their predicament: the **confused dyslexic** doesn't know she is dyslexic and struggles through life unaware of what's wrong; the **closet dyslexic** knows, but conceals the fact whenever possible, maybe even denies it to herself; and the **candid dyslexic** knows and is honest and open about her dyslexia.

As I'm sure you've figured, I think it's important to be open about dyslexia. Very simply, dyslexia means "trouble with words". It isn't caused by low intelligence, laziness, cultural disadvantage, emotional disturbance, allergies, birth trauma, or injury. Rather, it's neurological in nature and hereditary. It doesn't go away in adulthood, but is treatable. Children and adults can learn to read much faster and with better comprehension through reading classes specifically designed for dyslexics.

Marlene, at age 18, your focus is changing from dependence to autonomy. This can intensify the fear and doubt that have probably followed you since you began reading in first grade. The new and painful question you're faced with is "will I fail in life as I did in school?" You'll find your answer in the stories of many successful people who experienced the same self doubt, who may have felt humiliated by rude classmates or ignorant teachers, who wondered if the tremendous effort to keep up was worth it, and who also felt a deep and profound sense of inferiority because of dyslexia. You'll discover that others have suffered as you have and succeeded in spite of it.

Psychologist Alfred Adler wrote about children with learning disabilities and the danger of either developing failure lifestyles (a self-fulfilling prophecy established early on when they first failed at reading and writing) or opting for a life of overcompensation (reaching for extremely high fictional goals unattainable by any person).

Marlene, the next time you're handed a completely new script and asked to read it cold, tell the casting director about your dyslexia and that you would appreciate some extra time to work on it. Talent wins out in the long run, and when you're prepared and able to do your best work, you'll be respected and admired for overcoming a difficult problem with a beautiful performance. And to inspire you, from Ms. Nosek's book, here are some quotes from people you've heard of who are dyslexic:

Tom Cruise: "I became very visual and learned how to create mental images in order to comprehend what I read."

Ann Bancroft: "You learn to go where your strengths are and you go for them hard."

Thomas Edison: "We can derive the most satisfying kind of joy by thinking and thinking and thinking."

Albert Einstein: "When I am reading I only hear it and am unable to remember what the written word looks like."

Whoopi Goldberg: "We have a handicap and that handicap can be overcome."

Magic Johnson: "The looks, the stares, the giggles,...I wanted to show everyone that I could do better and that I could read."

Agatha Christie: "I was always the slow one in the family."

Neil Bush (son of George Bush): "I learned that through hard work I could overcome my handicap."

Hans Christian Anderson: "I was told I'd never become a writer."

As you can see, you're in very good company. We all have limitations, but in each of these cases, personal determination won out. It can for you too. If you really want to be an actress, don't let dyslexia stop you.

Chapter 23

Is It Shyness or Introversion?

Q. Dear Dr. Andrea, I've always wanted to be an actress but I'm very shy. Being shy gets in the way of a lot of things I want to do. How can I overcome my shyness so that I can have a better chance of becoming an actress?
Rita

A. Some very talented, successful actors and actresses consider themselves shy. In fact, people who want to overcome shyness often force themselves to face challenging situations, like public speaking or acting, to help them gain control of their shyness. But it's important to distinguish whether you're shy, which is a form of social anxiety, or you have an introverted nature, which may look like shyness, but is actually very different.

Shyness is a cluster of symptoms and signs that are caused by extreme selfconsciousness. Common signs of shyness include blushing, getting tongue-tied, making little or no eye contact and not talking. Often people who are shy are uncomfortable talking with people they don't know very well or have trouble starting a conversation. Shyness can be either **situational**, which means you're uncomfortable in many social situations, or **chronic**, where virtually all social situations are difficult. Both are social anxieties that can interfere with important aspects of your life and thwart your ability to accomplish tasks involving interaction with people. Shyness can be outwardly obvious or it can be well hidden and internally focused. Hidden shyness is masked by overly outgoing, aggressive, or overly sexy behavior. For example, Lawrence Olivier was quoted as saying that his friend Marilyn Monroe was actually very shy, although it's a little difficult to imagine.

The distinction between **introversion** and **extroversion** has been carefully studied by the great psychiatrist, Carl Jung. He wrote that these were modes of expression which were part of an individual's basic makeup. If you're an introvert, then your psychological energy flows inward. If you're an extrovert, psychological energy flows outward. Someone who shows a combination of these traits is called an **ambivert**. All three are inherent and part of one's nature. No value judgment should be made about one mode being superieor to another, although our American culture and education system strongly encourage extroversion, compared to India, for example, where introversion and introspection are prized. In fact, the world needs a balance of the qualities which both types provide.

Shyness is about a lack of self confidence. Introversion is about feeling more content when alone than with people and having more interest in solitude over socializing. A **shy introvert** almost always prefers solitary endeavors and is very uncomfortable in social situations. A **self confident introvert** (Einstein as an example) is perfectly contented to work alone, but is very capable of being in a group or speaking in public if required. Some actors are shy extroverts. You may fit this category because you feel anxious in social situations, yet feel a strong flow of psychological energy towards people and a strong motivation to overcome your shyness. The last category is the **self confident extrovert**, who has a genuine interest in others and flourishes among people.

Are we born with a tendency toward shyness in the same way that we have an innate tendency toward introversion or extroversion? Probably. Some children are shy from the very beginning. But because shyness may be part of your basic nature doesn't mean you can't alter it if you choose. Introversion doesn't usually cause an individual unhappiness, but shyness often does because it's limiting. There is a lot you can do to counter your basic tendencies and reshape them to suit you. This is where acting can be a vehicle to help you become the socially confident person you want to be. You can replace solitary activities with different acting venues. Acting, by its very nature, involves you with many people, all coming together for an artistic project.

It will be helpful to think of shyness as a habit. Although shyness may have a biological component, it's also a learned response. You withdrew as a little girl when you found it was difficult to cope in a social situation, and withdrawing eased your anxiety. Later, self consciousness followed by social withdrawal, became automatic. But the more you use avoidance, the more you strengthen it as a habit. To extinguish any type of habit or phobia, behavioral therapists use desensitization techniques to remove unwanted behaviors and replace them with useful ones.

Here are a few suggestions from a helpful book called *Conquer Shyness* by Frank J. Bruno, Ph.D. You may do these on your own, or have the help of a counselor who understands shyness and is experienced in using desensitization. Begin by visualizing situations that ordinarily make you anxious. Create movies in your mind in which you're outgoing and comfortable in social situations. Write a short story or script in which you're the major character. Create storylines putting yourself at the center of attention by initiating conversation, making the first step to reach out to someone, making a social phone call, dancing at a party, etc. Later, try out for a play or take a class in public speaking.

Each of these may cause a certain level of anxiety. When you've accomplished them in spite of the discomfort you feel, reward yourself. Give yourself credit for overcoming a hurdle. Take small steps, and as you succeed in those situations, move on to more difficult ones.

Shyness won't disappear by itself. Every time you give in to shyness, you strengthen the shyness habit. If you think of shyness as a permanent personality trait, you'll be unable to change. However, if you see it as an ineffective coping mechanism, as simply a behavior that you choose to change, you'll be able to do so. Challenge your usual way of thinking about yourself and others. Challenge the way you typically handle social situations. Practice being assertive. Maintain good eye contact with people with whom you're conversing. Practice confident body language. Learn to become less vulnerable to the opinions of others. And remember that self consciousness and shyness are not at all unusual. Many people feel the way you do, but not all have the fortitude to overcome it. One more very helpful tip from Bruce's book, is to adopt a "I'm more interested in you than in me" attitude. When you focus on the other person and whether he or she is feeling comfortable, you take your mind off yourself.

Many successful actors have refused to allow shyness to stand in their way. You can too.

Chapter 24

BECOMING A STUNT MAN

Q. Dear Dr. Andrea, I've always wanted to be a stunt man. I'm very athletic, race cars, do frozen waterfall climbing and water rafting, and have always liked doing things that are scary to other people. It gives me a rush that I can't explain. My wife is really against it because she feels it's too dangerous. We've had some major arguments about it, so we decided to ask you what you think.   *John and JoAnn*

A. Let me start by saying that I think it's a mistake for anyone to discourage the other's aspirations. Instead of arguments, why not conversation, so you can plan, compromise a little, and combine your visions for the future. You have every right to pursue your dream, but your wife may have an intuitive feeling that you like the thrill of the risk a little too much, and that desire for a "rush" could put you in danger. And, in fact, professional stunt people should be wary of that risk-taking passion too. You both need a lot more information, so I went to a member of the Board of Directors of the Stunt Men Association of Motion Pictures to help answer your question. George Fisher has been a stunt man and stunt coordinator for over 35 years. He works on an average of four movies a year, including work on *Titanic* which used stunt men and women from all over the world. His association gets inquiries from people all over the world, who see exciting stunt work in movies and want to pursue stunts as a career. He told me the following:

As a stunt coordinator, responsible for the safety of the stunt men, he cringes at the idea of "dare devils" who like to take unnecessary risks. A stunt must be planned, rehearsed, rigged properly, and carefully thought out in every way. All equipment, such as descenders, cables, airbags, fire fabrics, catchers, boxes, and break away railings, must be tested and retested. Twenty years ago George was one of the original developers of rigging and material for fires, making it possible to do some of the incredible fire scenes we see today.

It isn't easy to break into the world of stunts. There are only several hundred SAG union stunt people in California, mostly men, and approximately 40 women, some very small adults who often double for children, and occasionally, with exacting supervision, children who do some stunts. Often stunt men pass their skills onto their children, who then go into the business. To become qualified, you need to work out and train in as many areas as you possibly can, such as trampoline, motorcycle, climbing, rodeo, gymnastics, karate, and car racing. During this training period, it's highly recommended that you do several years of extra work, learning as you watch.

When you feel you're really ready, find out who the stunt coordinator is on the movie you're working on as an extra and simply hand him a picture and resume. Don't try to talk to him or "schmooze". Because stunt coordinators are likely to use people they already know, you have a much better chance of breaking in if you have a lot of special expertise in some area such as diving or helicopter hanging. When you finally get an opportunity to work, be prepared, cooperative, likeable, and a winner in every way. Never say you can do a stunt that you're unprepared to do.

Stunt people are SAG members and are paid the same daily or weekly rate that actors are paid. However, when working on a special or difficult stunt, like a car crash, stunt men are paid additionally for each take. They could rehearse for several days and then do the stunt all day long until the director has the scene exactly as he needs it. Non-union work can be more dangerous because the coordinator and all the stunt people are less experienced. A seasoned union stunt coordinator hires only very experienced stunt people for difficult or potentially dangerous situations. He anticipates weaknesses in the rigging and works with the special effects technician to avoid pitfalls.

But I'd like to address your need for challenges that the rest of us find hard to understand. Studies have been done which show that some people (mostly young males) have an inclination toward high risk behavior which is actually hard-wired into their brains and connected to the pleasure and arousal centers. These connections tend to decline with age. High sensation seekers seem to have a lower level of an important enzyme which regulates arousal. These people can handle high levels of stimulation without overload. If you're a high sensation seeker, you look for outlets to satisfy your need for stimulation. But, if you're driven to experience more risk and greater thrill, you put yourself (and others working with you) in jeopardy. If you want your wife's support in your pursuit, John, I think you'll have to find ways to temper your need for stimulation. She needs to know that you won't take unnecessary chances. In addition, the pros in the stunt world will insist that you be responsible and mature or the word will get out very quickly that you can't be trusted and could potentially put them at risk. Stunt work is a very skilled craft and a stunt person is an artist. Just because you can race a car doesn't mean you can stunt a car crash. The artistry is not how much risk you're willing to take, but rather in how carefully you rig the stunt ahead of time, making it as safe as possible, creating the illusion that the story requires and the director envisions.

Chapter 25

New York or LA?

Q. Dear Dr. Andrea, As you can see by the postmark, I live in Nevada and am willing to move to New York or LA for my acting career. I've visited both places but can't decide which would be the smartest move. It's such a huge decision that I'm frozen and can't make a move either way. What kinds of things do I need to know to make the best career move?

AG

A. As everyone knows, these two markets are the centers of the entertainment industry. Although some very impressive theater can be found in many cities, and film location shooting is done around the country, most television and film is written, produced, directed, and acted by talent living in or near LA and New York.

I've lived in both cities and love them both, yet am very aware of striking differences between them: differences in the way the entertainment business works, as well as the lifestyle and culture—not to mention the weather!

New York is fast paced, exciting, and filled with theater of all kinds, from the tiny hole-in-the wall places to the Broadway productions that are famous around the world. Television series, soap operas, situation comedies, television commercials, and feature films are being shot in studios and on-location in and around the city every single day. In New York many actors free lance, as opposed to signing with one agent. They find it a real plus having several agents working for them. Dealing with people in and out of the industry requires a little getting used to because (at the risk of making sweeping generalizations), most people who have lived there agree that New Yorkers are very direct, even blunt, and have little patience for the slower pace of out of towners! Many of us find directness a positive aspect of the New York personality because it's better to know how someone really feels and where you really stand.

If you're accustomed to open spaces and need to be surrounded by nature, you'll have a real problem living in the city. Small apartments cost a lot of money and many people don't even have a car because parking is an expense, and driving in the city can be slower than the subway, a taxi, or even walking. Because people both live and work in relative closeness, going to auditions is easier than in LA. You could go to one audition in New York, stop back at your apartment to change, then actually walk to your next audition. If you have some money, you can get a beautiful apartment with a view, or even better, you can find a home on Long Island, Connecticut, or New Jersey. Commuting on the Long Island Expressway has been known to drive some people completely crazy, so you can opt to take the train!

Los Angeles is the home of most of the major film studios and dozens of independent film production houses. Television production of every kind is done there, especially commercials, sit coms, series, and soaps.

In LA, actors don't freelance, but eventually sign a contract with one agent. You can have a separate agent for commercials, one for print, and one for theatrical. But many actors are signed with one full service agency for everything. Having several agents working for you without a contract, which is common in New York, isn't done in LA. Getting to auditions is a little more difficult because casting is done all over the city and in all the surrounding areas. It's virtually impossible to get around without a car and you'll need to leave more time to get to each audition than you would in New York. There's more "schmoozing" in LA, with some people telling you what you want to hear rather than telling you what they really think. As a result it can be difficult to know where you stand. But there are big hearted people living in LA. Because so many are transplants from other places, I find it a place where deep friendships are established, with people creating "friendship families" because real family members are often so many miles away. Of course California is one of the most beautiful places on earth, with Southern California possessing delightful weather almost all year long. This may seem unimportant, but once you've become accustomed to warm temperatures, sunshine, and year-round flowers and trees, New York may seem a little gray, if not down right harsh. And although LA is expensive, you have more options for finding a pleasant place with choices from city apartments to suburban houses to rent or buy.

To find agents, casting directors, and current productions, New York has *The Ross Reports* and LA offers *The Right Agent*, by Keith Wolfe, *The Agencies*, by Larry Park, and *The Working Actors Guide*. To keep you current about what's happening in the industry, New York has *Backstage* and LA has *Backstage West*. Both cities have the best training in the country, and the best photographers. Although there is tremendous competition in these markets, there is also incredible opportunity. If theater is your strength, New York has the edge. If feature film acting is your goal, Hollywood is the place. For soaps, sit coms, and commercials, both places have plenty of work in production.

To keep this in perspective, understand that breaking into the business on either coast will be one of the biggest challenges you ever take on. If you have an adventurous personality and are realistic about your pursuit, you'll have a great time. You'll do better, if you have a resume from your home town. If you have talent but little experience, you'll need to get into classes as soon as you arrive.

If you have a friend or relative in either of these cities, this might be the determining factor in your decision. Although you're bound to make friends, it's very nice to have someone to help you get around when you first arrive. Loneliness has caused more than a few actors to go back home to family and friends, not because they were discouraged, but because they felt a lack of connection. It will be important to somehow make one of these cities your home, with at least a few people you can spend time with and talk to. Since your home is Nevada, it would be easy and inexpensive to fly or drive home for holidays if you choose LA. These things can't be your main considerations, but they should play into your decision.

I know people who have come to LA from New York and simply cannot feel at home. New York is like no other place in the world. Whether you choose the Village, upper East Side, or another of the many distinctive neighborhoods, each little section has its own flavor and style. But California has a lot to offer, and can help you have a very nice life while you're pounding the pavement and working hard to get into the profession.

If you're adventurous, you could spend six months in one of these markets trying to find an agent, auditioning for as many casting directors as possible, and seeing what develops. If you don't have any luck, you can pack up and try the other. You wouldn't be the first actor who became bi-coastal!

Good luck!

Chapter 26

CHILDREN IN THE BIZ

Children in the entertainment industry face some unique challenges. Parents need to be prepared in order to ensure that it will be a rewarding and enhancing experience.

Q. Dear Dr. Andrea, I always wanted to be an actress but never pursued it seriously. Now my six year old daughter has shown interest in being on TV. She seems to be very talented and stands out in her acting classes. She has an agent who sends her out on auditions. Sometimes she wants to go and other times she doesn't. Should I insist that she go, to teach her responsibility? I don't want her to miss the opportunities that I missed, but sometimes it's a battle to get her there.   *Mrs. D.*

A. This is a big question, and one that I'm asked a lot. In LA and New York we're surrounded by studios, movie stars, and talk of huge salaries for jobs in commercials, TV, and films. Many parents and children see people they know working in the business and think, why not me? And, if you've always wanted to be an actress yourself and feel that somehow you missed your opportunity, your daughter's acting career may be more important to you than it is to her. So first you'll want to examine whether on some level you still want this for yourself. If you do have ambition and talent, maybe you should be going after your own dreams. If you know that becoming an actress is completely unrealistic for you, perhaps working in some other area of the business might be satisfying enough. After all, having a child doesn't diminish your need to find a satisfying outlet for your creativity.

Some people are lured by the possibility of money and fame. The fantasy of public adulation is the driving force that draws some to the industry. But it's important to teach our children what is worth pursuing and what isn't. I've actually had young children tell me they wanted to be movie stars so they could be rich and famous, and I've seen parents encourage these as goals. It's much wiser to help children discover what they love and what they're naturally good at. Children should be given the opportunity to learn what their strengths and talents are. Allowing children to sample acting, as well as music, the arts, athletics, and the sciences, gives them a well rounded education and helps them find a profession that will be rewarding later in life. This approach helps to ensure that your child will be successful. Financial security and the respect of others in your field are much more worthy and realistic goals than are fame. Still, it should be love for the work, not the possibility of fame that is the motivating force. Once you've assured yourself that your motives for having your daughter in the business are the right ones, we can focus on her.

I thought I would check with two well-respected children's agents about your daughter's lack of cooperation at auditions. Helen Garrett of the Judy Savage Agency has been an agent for 20 years and is the mother of Jimmy Garrett who played Lucy's son on *The Lucy Show*. She told me that occasionally her young clients express the need to decline auditions. The reasons include preferring to do something else, like a soccer match or feeling a little too pressured by the demands of successive auditions and the performance anxiety that comes with them. Helen always talked with her son about whether he wanted to continue, and because the desire was his rather than his mother's, he was usually enthusiastic. When occasionally he didn't want to go, they didn't go. But when it came time to sign the contract for *The Lucy Show*, she explained to him that once he signed, others would be counting on him and he would have an obligation to be at work. Once he understood, he decided to go ahead. This is a good example of helping children make choices and understand the consequences of those choices. Helen helped him understand the ramifications of doing a series, but allowed him to make the decision.

Pam Grimes of the Hervey/Grimes Talent Agency is an agent and the mother of Scott Grimes (*Party of Five*). She feels that if a child occasionally doesn't want to go to an audition, it's understandable and should not be forced. If, however, parents and child are struggling each time they get a call, it's a good indication that the child really doesn't enjoy the process, even if he or she hasn't directly expressed a dislike for it. In that case, I believe the child should take a break for at least six months. At the end of that time, you can both reassess whether it's a good idea to continue or put the idea aside permanently.

Sometimes children can't directly express what they're feeling. Children don't want to disappoint their parents. It will be especially difficult to say they don't want to do this when they realize how important it is to Mom or Dad. So they act out in indirect ways. Most children cannot express "this is too much pressure for me". Instead they may act hyper, unfocused, passive, angry, tired, or may behave rudely. When you assess whether your child is a good candidate for the profession, look not only at her natural talents, but also her temperament. Some kids handle the audition process better than others. Very sensitive children may take rejection to heart and find it difficult to maintain their self esteem if they go to many auditions, but get few jobs or callbacks. Other children take the whole thing in stride, partly because of the casual attitudes of their parents and partly because of their own psychological makeup.

If your child becomes successful in commercials, TV, or films, you have other issues to consider. In the midst of long hours on the set, schooling by tutors, lots of attention lavished on her and the knowledge that she could make more money than Mommy and Daddy, one of your biggest responsibilities is seeing to it that your child remains a child and lives as normal a life as possible. Remember, when dealing with agents and casting directors, you always have the final say regarding your child's career choices. Your decisions will be based not only on what's best for her career, but what's best for her as a developing person. Encouraging her to have friends and interests outside the business is very important, and helping your daughter find ways to do good deeds (like volunteering) will help to keep her well grounded in a world that can be glitzy and superficial. And preparing your daughter for the future includes teaching her to understand that child stars don't always become adult stars. A good education is a good safety net.

If being an actress is truly your daughter's interest, it can be a healthy and enhancing experience. I applaud you and other parents who are willing to devote the time and effort it takes to help your children explore their talents.

Chapter 27

COCAINE RECOVERY

Q. Dear Dr. Andrea, I'm twenty seven and have been using one kind of drug or another since I was twelve. I've been freebasing cocaine for awhile and sometimes use other drugs, and things are really getting out of control. My biggest problem is that I can't get help because I just can't let it get out that I have an addiction. It could ruin my career.

David

A. Isolation is the enemy of recovery. You're ashamed that you're losing your grip, but if you don't get help, it will ruin your career and your life. As you know, cocaine is a stimulant that keeps the body and mind running in high gear. Common sense should tell you that your system has to crash at some point. No one can sustain that kind of stimulation. If you're free basing, you have a profound dependence upon cocaine that is probably controlling every aspect of your life. And if you've been using crack, you are its slave. You're headed for destruction. I'm sure that you were drawn to cocaine because it gave you energy, lifted your spirits, and gave you a good feeling. These effects are caused by cocaine's influence on the reward center of the brain. It causes the release of dopamine, resulting in the euphoria you crave. Cocaine has worked its way into the lives of high achievers, entertainers, athletes, and the glamour crowd because many who are trying to make it in these areas, or who are trying to hold on to their place at the top, have insecurities that they may be unable to consistently work at peak performance. Many actually believe they can't do their best without cocaine. But the pleasures of cocaine are quickly erased by its trap. Following a high, there is a period of depressed mood (cocaine blues) and fatigue. The higher the highs, the lower the lows. The briefer the effects, the greater the addictive potential. Attempts are made to recreate the euphoria, leading quickly to tolerance, and acceleration of the dose needed. Higher doses result in restlessness, paranoia, and other unpleasant side effects.

There is no doubt that cocaine produces a profound psychological dependency, whether you snort, inject, or inhale. It was once thought that cocaine's dependence was primarily psychological because withdrawal from cocaine is different and faster than alcohol. But we've discovered that cocaine is one of the most quickly addictive of all drugs, and users experience the most intense cravings that can be caused by drugs. These cravings account for the destructive behavior associated with cocaine. The drug makes you want to take it again...and again...and again. After repeated use, the withdrawal period changes from "cocaine blues" to profound anguish. If you binge with cocaine, repeatedly taking dose after dose in increasingly higher amounts, you risk putting yourself through a full-blown paranoid psychosis including hallucinations. Acute cocaine poisoning can lead to profound stimulation of the central nervous system, convulsions, and even respiratory or cardiac arrest.

Of course, the majority of people who use cocaine do so with some self control. They spend a lot of money and delude themselves into thinking that cocaine will make them better, faster, smarter, and give them that "edge" they so desperately need to get through the day. Often, those who use the drug more conservatively do so because of its expense and then fill in with other drugs between cocaine sessions. By the time they develop an addictive cocaine syndrome, they're experiencing jittery side effects, so they use other substances, like marijuana or alcohol, to calm themselves.

My guess is that you probably started with marijuana and gradually found yourself trying more interesting and more dangerous drugs. Polydrug use is a very risky behavior that causes unimaginable changes in your central nervous system, your brain, and your entire chemical makeup. I think one of the most profoundly sad aspects of using drugs throughout adolescence and young adulthood is that the user has been mentally unavailable for key developmental stages. If you've been using something since you were twelve, we could say that on some level you're still twelve years old. Teenagers whose heads are clear are spending a good portion of their time developing a sense of identity, so they can successfully separate from their mothers and fathers. Through their activities, choice of friends, clothing, and other personal statements, they're learning to define themselves. This is a time when they should be learning to succeed at school, at sports, in the arts or music. They're learning how to deal with failures in a constructive way. They're also learning social skills they will need for the rest of their lives. And during this stage they are developing emotional autonomy, which will eventually allow them to break their dependency upon their parents. Heavy use of drugs through this developmental stage distances the young user from reality, creating an unreal world in which he or she lives.

Eric Erikson, a renowned psychiatrist who identified eight crucial developmental lifetime stages, believed that the identity stage of adolescence is the central developmental stage of life. The adult needs a unifying sense of identity in order to master the stages that follow. Identity confusion can cause someone to select a negative life identity. A lifetime marked by a lack of purpose, bad relationships, and missed opportunities is the result. As you can see, David, you have a lot of catching up to do. Proper treatment and intensive psychotherapy following cocaine detox can help you fill in the developmental deficiencies that you subjected yourself to.

One of your biggest concerns is being found out, so I'd like to address that issue and help you to see it differently. What happens with cocaine addiction is that users inevitably get sloppy because they're so desperate. It wouldn't be unusual for a user to take chances by snorting at work or leaving a pipe out where others could see it. The craving that drives you is more powerful than your good judgment and clouds your ability to behave normally. You might look edgy, restless, and overly stimulated, followed by a low, moody, pessimistic period. Additionally, heavy cocaine users often don't look healthy. They don't eat much and sometimes look too thin and colorless. Be honest with yourself, David. Doesn't this description sound at least a little like you? And do you really believe that no one knows? You have a better chance of earning the respect of those around you (not to mention finding some self respect), if you get treatment now.

Once you're in treatment, you're protected by rules of confidentiality, common to all treatment centers and individual therapists. The 12 Step programs are built upon anonymity. Typically, you can detox within a few days. But you must stay in a program, because within two or three months of being sober, relapses are very common. Mild depression or boredom following cocaine withdrawal can weaken one's resolve. Drug counselors and members of the 12 Step programs can help you through this period.

I asked a recovered cocaine user what advice she could offer. Without hesitation she stated that you must build a support system. You'll need to replace your old connections with new ones. People who are recovering help heal each other. With others who have succeeded, you'll learn to replace destructive choices with smart ones. You'll replace shame with self respect. Here are my recommendations:

1. Call Focus on Recovery Help line— 1- 800-274-2042

2. Get into an inpatient or daily outpatient treatment program.

3. Find a 12 Step program like Cocaine Anonymous and begin regular meetings.

4. If you mix drugs with alcohol, call AA and find a meeting near you.

5. Get into individual psychotherapy with a counselor who understands addiction.

6. Find a spiritual avenue that can give you focus on the meaning and purpose of your life and help shore up your strength during this recovery period. A church group might be very helpful.

7. Literally build a new family of supporters from these sources.

Believe me, there are thousands of people who have been there...done that. Thousands who were at the same crossroads have recovered. You can do this, David.

Chapter 28

Is It Love?

Q. Dear Dr. Andrea, I think I'm in love with my acting teacher. I keep trying to show him that I don't just want to be his student, but I can't seem to get through to him. I called him at home, I even dream about him. What else can I do?   *Heather*

A. I know how you feel. Almost everyone can remember falling for a teacher. This is usually a fleeting feeling that moves through us and evaporates as quickly as it appeared. You've told me very little about you or him, but my guess is that you're very young. We'll look at this from several different angles so that you can learn to handle these kinds of feelings.

Probably you don't know much about your teacher and maybe have never even seen him outside the classroom. This gives you a view of him that's very narrow and allows you to project qualities onto him that you want him to have. In other words, the less you actually know about someone, the easier it is to create in him the perfect love object. Honorable people are aware of this vulnerability in their students, patients, and interns and are careful not to take advantage of those who admire them.

Let's take a look at your own personal style of relating to men. If you have a strong sense of self and feel good about yourself, you can trust these feelings a bit better than if you're lonely, feel unsuccessful, or on some level just want and need someone to take care of you. Since you don't really know him, you may be infatuated with externals about your teacher: his blue eyes, his hair, his body, his knowledge of the craft of acting. These initial attractions are what draw us to people, creating a sexual chemistry, but they definitely aren't the things love is based upon. In and of itself, a crush on your teacher isn't bad, unless it draws your energy and your focus from your goals. You can waste a lot of precious time fantasizing about an unattainable love rather than putting that time to good use by working hard. This is actually one reason why people have an attraction to someone who may not be available. It's easier to dream of someone or something than it is to aggressively pursue a real life goal.

In some situations I'm not against a woman making one gesture toward getting to know a man better. If they're both students, have mutual friends, share a common interest such as a sport or hobby, or if they work together, but he is not her boss, and he is not married (that goes without saying), I see no problem with reaching out once. But knowing what I do about men, and having pretty good instincts about how men prefer the chase, I think a woman is asking for trouble if she pursues a man relentlessly, or pursues a man at all if he's in a position of authority with her, or has not given any real signals that he's interested in her. I know that women today commonly make the first move, assertively pursuing a guy and becoming sexually involved very quickly, being the "modern" woman in every way. I can tell you with great certainty that this isn't a very smart way to find love and to be cherished by a man. Thousands of years of human evolution are hard wired into men who still feel most manly (and most loving) when they've made the first step. Making the first move may get you a temporary sexual relationship, but not necessarily a serious one.

That doesn't mean you can't be friendly, warm, and encouraging. A woman who is confident, happy, secure with herself and friendly to a man is very appealing. Frankly, I'm not too concerned with the point of view that my approach is somehow using a double standard or is inequitable for women, because I know that smart women have been getting love and respect from men since the beginning of time. Insecure, weak women who chase and give when they don't get, end up with an empty plate. A smart woman can sense when a man has some interest in her and when he doesn't, and loses interest in him quickly if he doesn't return her feelings.

Now let's ask you a few questions, Heather, to help you see that your one-sided interest in your teacher isn't appropriate and could undermine his ability to teach you. Have you been attracted to men who are unavailable or unwilling to be monogamous? Are you excited by what your teacher represents rather than who he really is? Are you attracted partly because he seems uninterested? Do you push away men who are loving to you? Do you feel frightened or uncomfortable with someone who loves you?

If, in your childhood, you associated loving intimacy with being hurt, you may unconsciously choose men who won't allow intimacy to develop. If this is a pattern of yours and avoidance of intimacy is at the core of the issue, you will continue to make these kinds of choices until you release the hurt and pain from your past.

If you usually make good choices and have healthy relationships with men, you simply need to understand that your teacher doesn't see you the way you see him. Allow your energies to shift to other interests and friends, until one day the powerful feelings of infatuation that you felt for him have vanished. The ability to resist acting upon every feeling you have is a signpost of maturity.

Real love develops over time, as we learn to know a person and understand the real person behind the outward persona. Real love grows out of sharing common experiences and values. And real love is less about how you feel and more about how you behave toward your partner. Select carefully, Heather. Choose to give your loving energies to someone who will return that love.

Chapter 29
Out of Control Spending

Q. Dear Dr. Andrea, I'm actually making money, but I'm not keeping any of it. I've been making top figures for films that I'm in, but with all the help I get, I still don't seem to have money, and I'm at the point where I don't trust the people around me, or myself for that matter, to handle my money. I know I spend too much and hate to think about money.   *LP*

A. One of the things actors who become celebrities don't anticipate is how many people want to become indispensable to you and your career. Your agent takes 10%; if you have a manager, that's another 15%; then you'll probably have a lawyer, possibly a secretary, and a person who runs your household and personal affairs—all who will want to be paid well. And the busier you become, and the more career demands that are placed upon you, the more you'll be tempted to hand over the responsibility of your money to someone else, especially if you have a few insecurities about your ability to handle money. But you need to take control over this aspect of your success, because, even if you decide to get some help from a financial advisor, you don't want others making the final decision on where your money goes or how it should be invested. You could hire someone to handle your monthly bills and offer professional advice on investing, but if you're undisciplined and uneducated about making your money grow, you won't know until it's too late if you have good advisors or bad ones. Some may suggest that all you have to do is hire someone to control your spending; I say you must learn to resolve the problems you have with money.

In a book I'm particularly fond of, *Money Harmony* by Olivia Mellan, she lists money personality types: spenders, hoarders, avoiders, amassers, bingers, worriers, and money monks. The **spender** loves to buy whatever brings him pleasure and finds it difficult to save or delay gratification for long-term goals. The **hoarder** enjoys holding on to his money and finds it difficult to spend money on luxury items and immediate pleasures. **Avoiders** tend to avoid tasks of every-day money management, usually feeling incompetent about dealing with money. The **amasser** is likely to be very concerned with making lots of money and investing, sometimes with a preoccupation for money that precludes tending to other aspects of life. **Bingers** save and save and then blow it all at once. They sometimes binge buy, even when they don't have money to pay for the excessive spending. Organizations like Debtors Anonymous are very helpful for this money type. The **money monk** tries to avoid ever having too much money, believing that money is corrupting. Large amounts of money would make him feel guilty and unworthy. And the **worrier** frets about money, fearful that there won't be enough, often spends inordinate amounts of time computing where money will come from and where it will go. Energy is spent fearing terrible things that could go wrong, requiring a lot of money to correct.

As I analyzed these types, I realized that few of us fall into one specific type, but rather, because of the emotional charge associated with money, it might be more accurate to say that at different times in our lives, we move from one type to another. From what you've told me, I suspect that you're probably both spender and avoider (and perhaps binger)—a dangerous combination. If you spend too much, you can hire someone to police your spending, but if you're an avoider, you won't be willing to police the person you hired. Hollywood stories abound about stars who lost everything to careless or unscrupulous advisors. You certainly don't want to become one of those tragic stories.

Keep in mind that you should be at the top of the pyramid. Although it takes a team of players to help you maintain your career, you and you alone must take control and take responsibility for certain decisions. The others may be important to the entire working of your career, but they work for you and should get final approval from you for these decisions. Many actors whose strengths lie in their artistic talents are weak (or have little experience) in the business areas. They hand over the reins and slowly but surely lose control over their destiny. Why should a promoter or a manager take a larger piece of the pie than the talent it represents?

It's time to look honestly at why you're reckless with money. If you're making big salaries and find yourself without enough money, you not only give too large a percentage of it away to "the team", you may also squander the percentage that you keep for yourself. If you're unaccustomed to a lot of money, you may feel dizzy with the power you feel when you spend big. I'll bet you're spending more on all kinds of items associated with film success. After all, don't you want to show the world just how successful you really have become?

You may simply be inexperienced and a little careless, stemming from the belief that you will always have a lot of money. Or you might have some deeper reasons for spending too much money. Dealing with money responsibly means that you're acting like an adult. It means that you have to delay gratification and in fact sometimes deny yourself something you'd really like to buy. Some of the reasons you may overspend are: to elevate your mood; to feel more powerful; to satisfy a sense of entitlement; to calm anxiety; as a response to boredom; as a replacement for love and attention; as a substitute for sexual gratification; as a passive-aggressive way to express anger; or as an attempt to fill important and unmet childhood needs for basic trust, safety, or respect.

Resolving issues about spending too much money begins with an honest inventory of yourself. You may have to acknowledge your irresponsibility. You can develop a mature attitude about your money. Start by understanding the effect your parents had on your attitude toward money. What are your impressions of how your mother and father dealt with money? Did they concur, or did their money personality styles clash? Was there enough money to have a comfortable life or did the family do without and struggle to have basic needs met? Were your friends much richer or poorer than you? Is your disregard for proper handling of money a symptom of a rebellious nature? Do you flaunt your success? Because if that's it, I'd have to ask you what insecurities you are trying to hide? Do you feel inadequate to the challenges your career presents? Are you afraid of losing your new status?

At the core of all of this is actually a character issue. If you have skewed values and believe that the possessions money buys are the essence of the value of a man, you'll continue to spend to enhance your value and worth. If you believe that money is a tool that can be used to expand your options and to do good in the world, you'll carefully select the ways you'll spend that money.

These are all questions posed to get you thinking about what motivates you to behave in a way that is definitely not in your own best interest. Think on it, LP, and then take steps to change.

Chapter 30

FINDING A NEW PATH

Q. Dear Dr. Andrea, I stopped dancing professionally five years ago and since then I've lost a lot of my self confidence. My day job and other commitments interfere with my ability to pursue what I love, and I feel resentful and unhappy. I have activities that should be fun, but I can't seem to find my old self. I don't know what happened to the cheerful person I was. I'm 43 (although I don't look it or feel it) and wonder, am I just in the middle of a mid-life crisis? Your articles have really helped. Thanks.   Kim

A. You may be in the midst of a creative crisis as well as a mid-life crisis. There's a lot going on here, but I can tell you that giving up something you love leaves a space that needs filling with something that in some measure compensates for what you've lost. Especially in the entertainment industry, actors, musicians, and dancers find themselves forced to reevaluate their lives and often they need to change direction in mid-life. This is true whether they've experienced tremendous success or very little. You haven't mentioned why you gave up your dance career, but you wouldn't be the first dancer or athlete to come face to face with the fact that these are usually, by their very nature, short careers. Finding another outlet for your talent or discovering new talents will be your next challenge. I'm sure you know that artistic expressions such as dancing, singing, writing, painting, and acting fulfill an almost unexplainable creative need. Dancing, especially, is an art form that involves the full expression of the physical, emotional, and even spiritual elements of our nature. Shirley MacLaine, who is a wonderful actress and dancer, wrote about how much dancing has meant to her and how spiritually enriching it's been in her life. From my personal experience, I can tell you that a dance class that I've taken for years makes me very happy. Some say it's the endorphin high. I suspect it's more than that. Didn't dancing make you feel healthy and vigorous and very much in control of your life? If for some reason you can't continue, finding something to replace it is very important.

If you're spending time thinking about "what might have been", I'd like to suggest a unique book called *Going to Plan B* by Schlossberg and Robinson. It discusses the person with very high expectations who anticipated a certain outcome that never materialized: the actor who never got the big break; the director who had one hit movie, but not a second one; the couple who could never have children; the med school student who never became a doctor; the beautiful girl who never became a high fashion model. The world is filled with people who reach mid-life, look around and realize that life is very different than they imagined it would be. There may not have been huge disappointments, but a series of small expectations that simply did not materialize. These are called non-events, dreams that somehow got lost along the way. Something important to us, something we expected to happen, or someone we expected to become, simply did not happen. Many of these expectations developed while we were children, adolescents, or young adults. As each year passes, we continue to cling to outdated ideals of ourselves. We wonder why these events didn't occur, feel angry, and perhaps even cheated by life because they didn't. Yet, abandoning these dreams feels like quitting, and maybe even proves that we have given up on ourselves. Watching celebrities on television talk shows painfully points up what they seem to have that we do not. The pressure that we place on ourselves (and that others place upon us) is based on a social clock. If we don't marry, have children, or attain a certain success at work by a given age, we feel like failures. If we didn't make it as an actor, dancer, or singer in our twenties, whatever else we attempt seems like second best. We become obsessed with thoughts such as why don't I have more money, where is that beautiful house I was supposed to have, what happened to the career in show business that I was so determined to succeed at, and where is the admiration and respect of those around me that I hoped I would receive?

As you can see, although we don't talk about our non-events, they are deeply felt. And for some, they become the center piece of our psychological make up. On the surface, we live life, day by day, assuming our responsibilities, attending family functions and social events. Days turn into years, and all the while, hidden deep within us, is the sadness and grief we carry about the loss of our ideals. We anguish over the event that never happened. How agonizing it is to give up the dream, how hard it is to let it go. But only in the letting go do we free our energies and our creativity to look gratefully at what we do have and what else we may have the potential to do. We can all learn to cope creatively with these non-events, but most don't know how to. What may seem like a shattered dream may actually be an opportunity if we can identify the key non-events in our lives, honestly grieve their loss, and then begin to refocus and reshape the second half of our lives. Acknowledging the loss can be a turning point, freeing us to look in new directions or simply accept what is.

I'm always surprised at how often people don't know what kinds of pursuits would make them happy or how to substitute one pursuit for another. Even worse, many people don't even try to fill a void. We often have such a narrow look at our options that we can't even imagine replacing what we've lost. But loss is inevitable. We all experience small and great losses in our lives. Unless we replace those losses with new experiences, new people, and new passions, we're left feeling the emotions you feel now.

One of the developmental tasks of mid-life is to reassess past endeavors and select new ones. Developmentally speaking, mid-life is the age of generativity versus stagnation. That is, either we are productive, helping the next generation in some way, contributing something positive to the world, no matter how small, or stagnating, which usually involves a preoccupation with ourselves and a lack of direction and meaning in life.

The entertainment industry creates problems for people in mid-life because for the few whose professional dreams come true, there are thousands who don't quite reach theirs. The business can be frustrating because success is so often unattainable. Some have a taste of success only to lose it all while others strive and never succeed. If you don't have a higher purpose, it can be discouraging. You may be looking at your age, 43, and wondering where the time went, regretting that your career didn't continue, as you imagined it would.

One thing you might not realize is that 43 isn't what it used to be! If you don't look, feel, or act your age, it's because today, age 43 is young. You probably have more energy and certainly more opportunities than a 43 year old had in the past. Everyone should read *Passages* and *New Passages* by Gail Sheehy. I consider them to be classics on the subject of adult development and life stages. She points out that each life stage is longer than in past generations, giving the individual more time to fully and successfully negotiate the important tasks of each stage. This is partly because people have better health and live longer and also because more people engage in higher education, which takes from four to ten years beyond high school. So you can take comfort in the fact that you have about twice as much time to complete the tasks of your current life stage than the last generation did. You may have to rethink your life and your future to tailor it more to your liking. A woman in this culture, in these times, has so many interesting options.

Your job is to get on with the work of the second half of your life. It's a time of evaluation. Assess your relationships, your work, your personal strengths and weaknesses. Assume a grateful attitude. Find your mission for your present life stage. Use the guidance of religion, philosophy, psychology, or science to help you. Mastering a life transition, overcoming a life-changing crisis, and resolving the pain of your non-events prepare you for the next life passage. Coming to terms with the problems of the present stage makes the future an adventure unencumbered by unresolved issues.

Chapter 31

Taking Action

When I look back on each year that has passed, I always critique it—actutally give it a grade! Maybe it was a tough year, with a lot of stress or serious personal and professional issues with which to contend. Or, some years get an "A" because wonderful things happened, with exciting opportunities in my work, meaningful moments with my husband, and memorable times with my friends. Then I try to evaluate which events were beyond my control and which ones I created myself. It's true that next year is a blank slate and many of life's turns and twists are simply fate, but much of what happens to us (or doesn't happen) is the result of the choices we've made throughout the year.

It really isn't necessary to wait for the beginning of a new year to make resolutions. When you're ready to take action, you're ready to make some resolutions. I'll leave your personal resolutions in your hands, and focus on questions which will help clarify your career goals and evaluate whether you're doing all you can to be a working actor—or whether you really even want to be a working actor! Any time of the year you can make resolutions that will really make an impact on your future. Instead of making one all-encompassing resolution for the whole year, perhaps you'll make further progress by doing a "resolution of the month" plan! By breaking a large goal down into small manageable tasks, you'll feel encouraged when you check off the goal for one month and begin the next.

If you're an actor you must sometimes feel that agents, studios, lawyers, financial managers, and quirks of fate have more control over your destiny than you do. Perhaps one of your goals could be to incorporate the idea of taking as much control, in as many ways as possible.

Some of the following questions will help you create your own personal resolutions which will turn this year into one you can call an "A"!

1. How much do you really want this? Is acting a lark for you, is it something you dabble in or do you have a burning desire to work in this business? How well have you assessed your talent? How well can you handle the uncertainty that goes with it? Can you take it in stride when you get rejected? Realistic assessment of your talents and psychological makeup is a very worthwhile resolution and a good beginning.

2. Are you fully prepared for the "business" side of acting? Do you have an answering machine and a beeper or a cell phone so that you can be reached for an audition? Do you have a *Thomas Guide* so that you can arrive at those auditions on time and with as little stress as possible? Are your pictures and resumes up to date and professional looking?

3. Are you prepared with a strong dramatic scene, a comedic scene, and one good monologue? Do you have a demo reel or voice over tape?

4. Do you continue to study? Do you see good movies and go to the theater?

5. Do you have a realistic idea of how much work is involved ? Are you reliable, punctual, and are you always prepared? Are you disciplined?

6. Do you know your type and are you comfortable with it? Do you know your strengths and how to emphasize them? Have you made the most of your appearance? Do you have enough information about hair and makeup so you will look good for auditions?

7. Of course, I think it's valuable to look inward for the most important resolutions. Too many of us blame others, a bad economy, bad luck...anything we can point a finger at, rather than examine how we've played the dominant role in our own destiny. Our attitudes and outlook color the world around us and cause us to either take the right action, the wrong action, or no action. Much of what happens to us is of our own doing.

Any one of these would be a good starting point for worthwhile resolutions, but it takes an inner determination to make them happen.

We all have good intentions, but there are two obstacles which keep us from staying on track. First are day-to-day life events which must be tended to and which divert us from our plan—such as family responsibilities and our "day" job- you know, the one that pays the bills! It doesn't make sense to resent these facts of life. After all, you're fortunate if you have family and job, which are the backdrop, the foundation from which you can then pursue your career. Second is the innate drive to revert to what we are comfortable with. As powerful as your desire may be, there is probably a little tug from within that wants you to stay in your comfort zone! So, first choose a resolution that you have a strong desire for and one that can be fairly easily accomplished, given your particular life. The biggest mistake is to try to fit in all your career resolutions at once, setting yourself up for failure. One resolution each month for the whole year will make it manageable and rewarding. Tackle something that is doable and when you have accomplished that one, select one more and so on. Then, consider the obstacles you anticipate and plan how you will deal with them. Get creative about problems that present themselves, and believe me, problems will arise.

Make your master plan visual—either by keeping a journal for the year or designing an action board. My own action board, which I've had for years and which helped me get through graduate school, is simply a large piece of cardboard on which I place colored post-its. Each post-it is marked and represents a small step to a larger goal. As each step is accomplished, pulling off that post-it brings a feeling of satisfaction. Your own action board can include personal and professional categories.

Even if your resolution is as simple as finding more time to have fun, you've verbalized or written a desire, elevating it from a simple wish to a definable step forward. Make it happen this year. Take the steps necessary to live your dream, just one small resolution each month! Imagine where you'll be next year at this time!

Index

Bibliography

BackStage West/Drama-Logue. California: BPI Communications, Inc., 2000.

BackStage. New York: BPI Communications, Inc., 2000.

Claude-Pierre, Peggy. *The Secret Language of Eating Disorders*. New York: Random House, 1997.

Csikszentmihalyi, Mihaly. Flow, *The Psychology of Optimal Experience*. New York: Harper & Row, 1990.

Drew, Jane, Myers. *Where Were You When I Needed You, Dad?* California: Tiger Lily Publishing, 1992.

Dunn, Gloria. *From Making a Living to Having a Life*. California: Violin Publishing Company, 1999.

Henry, Kimberly, A. and Heckaman, Penny, S. *The Plastic Surgery Sourcebook*. California: Lowell House, 1997.

Hill, Andrea. *Performance Anxiety, Shame and the Ego Ideal*. Doctoral Dissertation, California Graduate Institute, 1993.

Hirschmann, Jane, R. and Munter, Carol, H. *Overcoming Overeating*. New York: Ballantine Books, 1989.

Jampolsky, Lee. *Healing the Addictive Mind*. California: Celestial Arts, 1991.

Kabat-Zinn, , Jon. *Wherever You Go, There You Are. Mindfulness Meditation in Everyday Life*. New York: Hyperion Publishing, 1994.

Kerr, Judy. *Acting is Everything*. California: September Publishing, 1981.

Mellan, Olivia. *Money Harmony*. USA: Walker Publishing Company, Inc., 1995.

Morris, Eric. *Acting From the Ultimate Consciousness*. California: Ermor Wnterprise, 1988.

Nosek, Kathleen. *Dyslexia In Adults*. Texas: Taylor Publishing Company, 1997.

Potter-Effron, Ron. and Potter-Effron, Pat. *Letting Go of Anger*. California: New Harbinger Publications, Inc., 1995.

Ratey, John, J. and Johnson, Catherine. *Shadow Syndromes*. New York: Random House Inc., 1997.

Rosenbluth, Michael. and Yalom, Irvin, D. *Treating Difficult Personality Disorders*. California: Jossey-Bass Inc., 1996.

Ross Report. New York: BPI Communications, Inc., 2000.

Schlossberg, Nancy, K. and Robinson, Susan Porter. *Going To Plan B*. New York: Simon & Schuster, Inc., 1996.

Sheehy, Gail. *New Passages*. New York: Random House, Inc., 1995.

Sheehy, Gail. *Passages*. New York: E.P. Dutton & Company, Inc., 1976.

Slipp, Samuel. *The Teaching and Practice of Object Relations Family Therapy*. New Jersey: Jason Aronson, Inc., 1993.

Park, Lawrence. *The Agencies*. California: Acting World Books, 2000.

Wolfe, Keith. *The Right Agent*. California: Silver Screen Publishing, 2000.

Working Actor's Guide. California: Aaron Blake Publishers. 2000